Handling Words 2

HOW TO READ AND SPELL THOSE LONG, HARD WORDS

Rebecca Super

CAMBRIDGE Adult Education
Regents/Prentice Hall Englewood Cliffs, NJ 07632

Editorial/production supervision
  and interior design: *Christine McLaughlin Mann*
Acquisitions editor: *Mark Moscowitz*
Executive editor: *James W. Brown*
Project editor: *Julie Scardiglia*
Copy editor: *Ann Graydon-Pietropinto*
Prepress buyer: *Ray Keating*
Manufacturing buyer: *Lori Bulwin*
Scheduler: *Leslie Coward*

©1993 by REGENTS/PRENTICE HALL
A Division of Simon & Schuster
Englewood Cliffs, New Jersey 07632

Printed in the United States of America
10 9 8 7 6 5 4 3 2 1

ISBN 0-13-946641-X

Prentice-Hall International (UK) Limited, *London*
Prentice-Hall of Australia Pty. Limited, *Sydney*
Prentice-Hall Canada Inc., *Toronto*
Prentice-Hall Hispanoamericana, S.A., *Mexico*
Prentice-Hall of India Private Limited, *New Delhi*
Prentice-Hall of Japan, Inc., *Tokyo*
Simon & Schuster Asia Pte. Ltd., *Singapore*
Editora Prentice-Hall do Brasil, Ltda., *Rio de Janeiro*

Contents

iv

v

Acknowledgments

Acknowledgment is given, with gratitude, to Ypsilanti (Michigan) Adult Education and to the students in my class who helped test these pages. Special acknowledgment goes to my husband, Robert who proofread, suggested, and encouraged.

Dictionaries: *Webster's New World Compact School and Office Dictionary,* 1982, Simon & Schuster
Webster's New World Dictionary of the American Language, College Edition, Simon & Schuster
Scott Foresman Intermediate Dictionary

Word list: *Capricorn Rhyming Dictionary,* by Bessie Redfield, 1939, Perigee Books (Putnam Publishing Group)

To the Teacher/Tutor

In *Handling Words 2,* students will continue to use the methods of decoding words they learned in *Book 1*—that is, using phonic, structural, and context clues and memorizing sight words. No new aspects of decoding are introduced in this book. *Book 2* consolidates the many skills presented in *Book 1* and applies them to new phonic elements introduced in an orderly progression. Words containing phonic elements beyond the students' vocabulary are not used in instructions or exercises until the elements are formally introduced in a chapter. In order to build confidence in the student, vocabulary words containing the new element start with the familiar and proceed to the less common. Then, at the end of each chapter, in "Handling Words . . . Lightly," students practice what they have just learned, by reading words in the context of business, entertainment, politics, science, and education. The vocabulary of this book was selected from sources as diverse as the daily newspapers (advertisements, entertainment, medical articles, etc.), G.E.D. preparation books, telephone and zip code directories, and the shelves of the supermarket. It is expected that students finishing these two books will have developed skills that are almost second-nature in reading and spelling words they need for the G.E.D., further educational training, and coping with the world in which they live. They will recognize which words present problems for spelling and pronunciation and know when and how to use the dictionary.

On Using the Book

Do the lessons DAILY, if at all possible.

MODEL the sound and EXPLAIN the construction. Students learn by the three main senses for language—hearing, sight, and kinesthetic sense—but they also learn by reasoning, by understanding what the word construction is all about.

BE FLEXIBLE, particularly in accepting answers on where a syllable break comes. Dictionaries don't always agree; and as long as no more than one vowel sound is included in a syllable, there should be no problem. Since we come from a diverse population, differences in pronunciation must be recognized.

Have students WRITE even more now than they did in *Book 1*. Dictation, by teacher or fellow-student, is very important. Have them use the words in sentences and write paragraphs, perhaps around some topics in the "Handling Words . . . Lightly" sections.

PROMOTE COMPREHENSION by using the "Handling Words . . . Lightly" sections to discuss word value and use.

MOVE ON if a student knows the material. You can "test" readiness for moving on by having the student write and by hearing the student read some of the "less-common" words and accompanying sentences. Test decoding readiness, also, by hearing the student read G.E.D. Practice Test words in the Appendix for the chapter in question.

PROVIDE MORE PRACTICE for students who need it. A rhyming dictionary is a very useful tool for finding new words suitable for extra practice.

Brief Review of *Book 1, Handling Words*

This section is for those students who have not recently worked in *Handling Words, Book 1*. This review is not a substitute for *Book 1*; it is only a refresher course in the most basic elements and patterns of English words covered in the first book. For learning the finer points and necessary practice, you should go back to the first book. If you are already well acquainted with *Book 1*, move directly to Chapter 1.

Consonants

1. The Consonants

b, c, d, f, g, h, j, k, l, m, n, p, q, r, s, t, v, w, x, y, z are the consonants—letters that are not vowels (*a, e, i, o, u,* and *y*). The letter *y* can be either a vowel (**my**) or a consonant (**yes**).

2. The letter *q*

q always has *u* after it in English words. The sound of *qu* is *kw*: **queen, quick, quiet.**

3. The Two Sounds of *c* and *g*

The letter *c* has no sound of its own. It has the hard sound of *k* in most words: **can, cup, pick.** But if the vowels *i, e,* or *y* follows *c*, the sound is *s*, a soft sound: **city, cent, Nancy.** The dictionary respells *c* with *k* or *s*: **can** (kan), **cup** (kup), **city** (sit′ e̅), **cent** (sent), **Nancy** (nan′ se̅).

The letter *g* is usually hard, as in **go, game,** or **gun.** In most words in which *i, e,* or *y* follows *g*, the soft sound is that of *j*: **gin, gents, gym.** The dictionary respells the soft *g* as *j*: **gin** (jin), **gents** (jents), **gym** (jim).

4. Consonant Pairs

Some consonants come in pairs and have only one sound although you see two letters: *sh* (ship), *ch* (chip), *th* (thanks), *ck* (back), *ph* (phone), an *f* sound, and *gh* (laugh), another *f* sound. These pairs are treated as if they were one letter and are rarely separated when you break words into syllables.

5. Blends

Some consonants appear together in a pattern, but each letter keeps its sound. These are the **blends.**

1. Beginning blends: *bl* (black), *cl* (clip), *fl* (flip), *gl* (glad), *pl* (plan), *sl* (slip), *spl* (split), *br* (bring), *cr* (crop), *dr* (drip), *fr* (fresh), *gr* (grab), *pr* (press), *scr* (scrape), *shr* (shrill), *spr* (spring), *tr* (trip), *thr* (throw), *sc* (scale), *scr* (scream), *sk* (skate), *sl* (slap), *sm* (smile), *sn (snake)*, *sp* (spill), *spr* (spring), *squ* (squeal), *st* (state), *str* (string), *sw* (swing).

2. End blends: *ld* (fold), *lf* (self), *lk* (milk), *lt* (wilt), *nch* (lunch), *nd* (end), *ng* (sing), *nk* (sink), *nt* (sent), *sk* (risk), *sp* (clasp), *st* (last) *dge* (judge), *ft* (left), *mp* (lamp), *pt* (lept). There are a few more. When breaking words into syllables, the blends are usually kept together.

6. Silent Letters

Some letters in some words do not sound at all: **write** (silent *w*), **know** (silent **k**), **sign** (silent *g*), **guess** (silent *u*).

The Vowels: *a, e, i, o, u, y*

Most vowels studied in *Book 1* have two sounds. The vowels are said to be *long* or *short:*

A *short* vowel is said very quickly. The sound is very light: **hit, bed, bad, hot, cup.** In most words, the short vowel is in the middle of the word or word part. The *u* sound as in **cup** is heard in some *o* words: **son, does, come.** Most dictionaries show short vowels with no mark.

The *long* vowel sound is made when you say the letter's name. You hold a long vowel for a longer time: **like, Pete, cake, bone, rule.** The silent *e* on the end of these words makes the vowel coming before it *long*. In most words, a vowel at the end of a word or word part is *long*. Other ways of spelling long vowels are:

i	*e*	*a*	*o*	*u*
igh (high)	**ea*** (eat)	**ai** (rain)	**oa** (boat)	**ew** (new)
y (my)	**ee** (feet)	**ay** (may)	**ow** (slow)	**eu** (feud)
	ie (niece)			
	ey (kidney)			

*In a few, common words, **ea** has the short **e** sound: **head, weather, dealt.**

The Long Vowel Mark   Most dictionaries show the long vowel with a short line over the letter: līke   sēat   māde   hōpe   tūne.

Syllables and Accents

1. Syllables

A **syllable** is a word or a part of a word that has a vowel sound. Some syllables are complete words and some are not: *I, a, ing, er, sad, ly, con, tin, ue*—one vowel sound in each. When you add endings such as *ing, ed, er, es, ful, ness,* or *est*, you are adding syllables to a word.

2. Syllable Rule: Compound Words

When two words are written together, you have a compound word: **handbag.** You break the compound word between the two words, **hand** and **bag.**

3. Syllable Rule: The *le* Syllable

This syllable *(le)* is one of a kind because it has no vowel sound. Break an *le* word so that one consonant is with *le: can dle.* When a word has *ck* and ends in *le*, break the word after *ck: pick le.*

4. Syllable Rule: Two or More Consonants After the First Vowel

In words with more than one consonant after the first vowel, break the word between the first two consonants: **sudden**—*sud den*.

5. The Accent Mark and the Schwa

Dictionaries put the accent mark (′) after (or just before) the syllable that is said more loudly than the rest of the word: **hel′ met**. In longer words, there may also be a lesser accent. This mark is shown in lighter print: **epidemic** ep′ i dem ′ ic). When reading a word you are not sure of, you often must try accenting one part of a word and then another. If you still don't know the word, go to the dictionary for help.

In many words, the dictionary replaces the vowel that is not in the accented syllable with this little mark, ə, called the *schwa:* **hel′ mət.** The schwa sound is about the same as the short *u* in **up**. It is the sound you make when you say many unaccented vowels. In some words the unaccented vowel is shown as completely dropped: **reason** (rē′ z'n). In still other words, an unaccented vowel will have the short *i* sound: **repeat** (ri pēt′).

6. Syllable Rule: One Consonant After the First Vowel

If only one consonant comes right after the first vowel, break the word after the vowel and try it out. In most words, a vowel at the end of a syllable is "long" (the letter's name is heard as you say the vowel). If you don't know the word, try breaking it *after* the consonant, making the vowel closed-in by other letters or "short." If you still don't know the word, use the dictionary.

7. Split Vowels

In some words, pairs of vowels must be split into separate syllables: *ue* (fu / el), *eu* (mu / se / um), *iu* (sta / di / um), *ui* (ru / in), *ua* (tru / ant), *ia* (tri / al), *eo* (ne / on), *oe* (po / et), *ea* (i / de / a).

8. The Shifted Accent

In some words the accent shifts from one syllable to another,
depending on the job the word does in the sentence: You get
pro′duce from a farm. The farmers **produce′** many different crops.

In some words, the accent shifts when a suffix / ending is added:
med′icine   medic′inal

9. Syllable Rule: Prefixes / Beginnings

A prefix is a letter or letters added to the beginning of a word to
change its meaning: **like, dislike.** A prefix that has a vowel sound is
a separate syllable. In some words the prefix has become so woven
into the word that you cannot drop it and still have a word (**district**).
For this reason, the term "prefix / beginning" is used in these books.
Listed below are the prefixes / beginnings studied in *Book 1*: *anti,
com, con, dis, de, en, ex, in, mid, mis, non, pre, pro, re, sub,
trans, un, under.*

10. Syllable Rule: Suffixes / Endings

A suffix is a letter or letters added to the end of a word to change the
meaning: **fish, fishing.** As with prefixes, the suffix in some words
has become so woven into the word that it can't be dropped; in
traffic, you won't have a word if you drop *ic* since *traff* is not a
word. For this reason, the term "suffix/ending" is used in this book.
In most words, the suffix is a separate syllable and in most words
with a suffix/ending, the syllable break comes just before the
suffix/ending. The following are suffixes studied in *Book One*: *able,
ade, age, al, ance, ant, ate, ed, en, ence, ent, er, es, est, ful, ible,
ic, ing, ise, ize, ish, ism, ist, ity, ive, less, ly, ment, ness, y.*

Spelling and Words with Suffixes/Endings

1.

Add *es* to words ending in *ch, sh, s, x,* or *z:* **beaches, dishes, glasses, mixes, whizzes.** To words ending in other letters, simply add *s.*

2.

In words ending in *y*, change *y* to *i* before adding suffixes/endings that have a vowel as the first letter (*es, ed, er, age,* etc.) This is not true of adding *ing*. If a vowel comes just before *y*, just add *s.* Consonant before final *y:* **copy, copies, copied, copier** but **copying.** Vowel before final *y:* **play—plays, played, player,** and **playing.**

3.

Drop the final *e* before adding a suffix/ending that starts with a *vowel.* Keep the *e* if the suffix/ending begins with a consonant: **like, liking   store, storage   pack, packing**

4.

Double the last letter of a word before adding a suffix/ending that starts with a vowel, *if* the vowel in the base word is **short** and *if* there is only **one** letter following that vowel: **hit, hitting**—but **fill, filling.**

5.

Double the last letter of longer words when the accent is on the *last* syllable and only *one* letter follows the last vowel: **regret′, regretted.**

Chapter 1
er ir ur

> *er* as in **her** (hʉr)   *ur* as in **fur** (fʉr)
>
> *ir* as in **bird** (bʉrd)   *er* as in **very** (ver′ ē)
>
> *er* as in **here** (hir) and **pier** (pir)

Sound and Spelling

1. The sound of *er* as in **her**, *ur* as in **fur**, and *ir* as in **bird**

When **r** follows a vowel, the sound of the vowel changes in most words. The **e** in **he** and **head** is different from the sound made by *er* in **her**. The **i** in **bit** and **bite** is different from the sound made by *ir* in **bird**. And the **u** in **fuss** and **fume** is different from the sound made by *ur* in **fur**.

> The sounds of *er* (**her**), *ur* (**fur**), and *ir* (**bird**) are the same in many words.

Write the words that have the same vowel sound and the same consonant ending as the numbered words.

bur	curd	her	herd	hurt	irk	jerk
skirt	spur	spurt	stir	third	Turk	

1. fur   *bur*   *her*   *spur*   *stir*

2. bird   _____   _____   _____

3. shirt   _____   _____   _____

4. clerk   _____   _____   _____

Read sentences with some of these words and others with *er, ur, ir*.

1. The <u>stern</u> father told his son, "You <u>hurt</u> your sister, and that <u>irks</u> me."

2. My picture of a <u>bird</u> in the <u>birch</u> tree was just a big <u>blur</u>.

3. The <u>clerk</u> did not make a <u>slur</u> about <u>Turks</u>.

4. A cowboy slept in the upper <u>berth</u>, his <u>spurs</u> still on his boots and sticky <u>burs</u> all over his pants.

5. The boss would watch us from his <u>perch</u> on the balcony to see that we didn't <u>shirk</u> our duty. What a <u>jerk</u>!

Longer, Common Words with *er* (as in **her**)

Write in *er* and read the words.

1. p _er_ son
2. mod __ __ n
3. p __ __ fect
4. s __ __ vant
5. th __ __ mos
6. sh __ __ bet
7. p __ __ mit
8. s __ __ mon
9. lant __ __ n
10. v __ __ dict
11. al __ __ t
12. sev __ __ al

Longer, Common Words with *ur* (as in **fur**)

Write in *ur* and read the words.

1. p __ __ chase
2. m __ __ der
3. n __ __ sery
4. c __ __ rent
5. b __ __ den
6. dist __ __ b
7. s __ __ vive
8. st __ __ dy
9. h __ __ ry
10. f __ __ nish
11. Sat __ __ day
12. s __ __ render

Longer, Common Words with *ir* (as in **bird**)

Write in *ir* and read the words.

1. th __ __ ty
2. b __ __ thday
3. d __ __ ty
4. Sh __ __ ley
5. f __ __ sthand
6. squ __ __ rel
7. th __ __ sty
8. g __ __ dle
9. conf __ __ m
10. V __ __ go
11. th __ __ teen
12. sk __ __ mish

2. The Sound of *er* as in **very**

> This is the sound most people hear in **fair, hair, air**.

Read the words.

there   cherry   berry   ferry   terry   sherry

Longer, Common Words with *er* (as in **very**)

Write in *er* and read the words.

1. J __ __ ry
2. sh __ __ iff
3. h __ __ ring

4. m __ __ it
5. inh __ __ it
6. __ __ rand

7. G __ __ ald
8. __ __ ror
9. st __ __ ile

3. The Sound of Short *i* as in **here** (hir), **spirit** (spir′ it), and **pier** (pir)

> This is the same sound you hear in such common words as **beer, cheer, queer** and **ear, year, dear**.

Write in *er* and read the words giving *er* the short *i* sound.

1. h __ __ e   2. m __ __ e   3. sev __ __ e   4. sinc __ __ e   5. h __ __ o

Write in *ir* and read the words giving *ir* the short *i* sound.

1. sp __ __ rit   2. m __ __ ror

Write in *ier* and read the words giving *ier* the short *i* sound.

1. p __ __ __
2. p __ __ __ ce

3. f __ __ __ ce
4. cash __ __ __

5. front __ __ __
6. brass __ __ __ e

4. Spelling *ur, ir,* and *er* Words

> You can't tell how to spell these three pairs just by hearing the words. You have to remember to go to the dictionary. Sometimes it takes three tries before you find the word you want, or the name you are looking for in the telephone book.

Write the words and add *ing* and *ed*.

> **Remember:** Drop the final *e*.

1. curl   *curling* , *curled*
2. jerk   _____ , _____
3. confirm   _____ , _____
4. murder   _____ , _____
5. reserve   _____ , _____
6. surprise   _____ , _____

Write the word and add *s* or *es*.

> **Remember:** Change *y* to *i* before adding *es* when *y* follows a consonant. Write *es* after words ending in *sh, ch, s, x, z*.

1. berry _____
2. hurry _____
3. curfew _____
4. church _____
5. flurry _____
6. girdle _____
7. nursery _____
8. curse _____

Syllables and Accents

1. Writing Words in Syllables

> *er, ir ur*, in most words, are not split.

Write the syllables in the blanks and put in the main accent mark.

Some of the words have prefixes/beginnings and suffixes/endings.

> **Remember:** *c* has the soft sound of *s* when *e, i,* or *y* comes after it. *g* has the soft *j* sound when *e, i,* or *y* follows it, in most words.

1. merchandise   *mer´   char   dise*
2. government   _____ _____ _____
3. funeral   _____ _____ _____
4. survival   _____ _____ _____
5. perishable   _____ _____ _____ _____
6. experiment   _____ _____ _____ _____
7. maternity   _____ _____ _____ _____
8. circular   _____ _____ _____
9. miracle   _____ _____ _____
10. circulate   _____ _____ _____
11. urgency   _____ _____ _____
12. allergy   _____ _____ _____

2. *er* and *ir* Prefixes/Beginnings

per   (meaning <u>through</u>, <u>throughout</u>, <u>thoroughly</u>, <u>by</u>) as in **permit**

super   (meaning <u>above</u>, <u>over</u>, <u>extra</u>) as in **superman**

inter   (meaning <u>between</u>, <u>among</u>) as in **interact**

circum   (meaning <u>around</u>, <u>about</u>) as in **circumstances**

ir   (meaning <u>not</u>; used before *r*) as in **irresistible**

Write the words in syllables and put in the main accent mark.

1. perhaps   _____ _____
2. supervise   _____ _____ _____
3. permanent   _____ _____ _____
4. circumstances   _____ _____ _____ _____
5. interstate   _____ _____ _____
6. superintendent   _____ _____ _____ _____ _____
7. intervene   _____ _____ _____
8. persecute   _____ _____ _____
9. circumference   _____ _____ _____ _____
10. supersonic   _____ _____ _____ _____
11. irresistible   _____ _____ _____ _____ _____
12. irresponsible   _____ _____ _____ _____ _____

Read these words and others with the new prefixes/beginnings in sentences.

1. The highway department will not <u>supervise</u> building the <u>interstate</u>.

2. <u>Perhaps</u> the new <u>superintendent</u> will make some big changes.

3. The <u>circumstances</u> of the army camp were so bad the general had to <u>intervene</u> to save the men.

4. A general who lets his officers <u>persecute</u> prisoners is <u>irresponsible</u>.

5. The <u>supersonic</u> plane, which travels faster than sound, is a <u>permanent</u>
   part of the air force.

6. The <u>circumference</u> of the world is the distance around it.

7. They were on a diet but found the chocolate cake <u>irresistible</u>.

8. Wearing a bathing suit to church would be an act of <u>irreverence</u>.

3. An *er* Suffix/Ending

ery (meaning <u>a place to do something</u>, <u>an act</u>, <u>a product</u>, <u>a group of things</u>,
<u>a state of being</u>) as in **bakery**

> *ery* has two syllables: *er y*.
> The main sound is *er* as in **her**.

Write the words in syllables.

1. bakery _____ _____ _____

2. lottery _____ _____ _____

3. bribery _____ _____ _____

4. grocery _____ _____ _____

5. shrubbery _____ _____ _____

6. delivery _____ _____ _____
   _____ _____ _____

7. recovery _____ _____ _____
   _____ _____ _____

8. upholstery _____ _____ _____

4. The Shifted Accent

Study the words for meaning.

*desert′	to leave someone	des′ ert	a dry place
permit′	to give your OK	per′ mit	a license
perfect′	to make right	per′ fect	exact, complete
convert′	to change	con′ vert	one who has changed faith
insert′	to put something in		
		in′ sert	the thing that is put in something

*The dessert you eat is spelled with an extra **s**.

Put in the accent marks in the underlined words.

1. There are snakes in the desért. Don't desért your friends.

2. He won't permit me to go. I need a permit to build on to the house.

3. Nobody is perfect. We are trying to perfect our skills on the computer.

4. You can't convert me to your way of thinking. She is a convert to the Catholic church.

5. This insert in the newspaper is about the sale. I must insert a sentence in this letter.

8

5. Word Building

Put a slash between the syllables and put in the main accents. Read the sentences.

> ☞ *Remember:* In some longer words, the accent shifts to another part when a prefix/beginning or suffix/ending is added.

1. **per/son   personal   personally   personalize   personality**

   What <u>person</u> would hit a sick child? <u>Personally</u>, I think the singer has a great <u>personality</u>. Putting your name on something <u>personal</u> will <u>personalize</u> it.

2. **experiment   experimental   experimentally**

   The <u>experiment</u> in the lab was a success. He worked on an <u>experimental</u> airplane. <u>Experimentally</u>, the bomber was a flop; they must try again.

3. **reverse   reversible   irreversible**

   Put the car in <u>reverse</u>. Her raincoat is a <u>reversible</u>, useful in dry as well as wet weather. The damage to the river after the oil spill was <u>irreversible</u>.

4. **conserve   conserving   conservative   conservatively**

   You must <u>conserve</u> gas and heat. The report was very <u>conservative</u> about spending money on <u>conserving</u> gas in cars. <u>Conservatively</u> speaking, the death toll from the quake was low.

6. Split Vowels

iu

Write the words in syllables.

1. delirium ____ ____ ____ ____

2. geranium ____ ____ ____ ____

3. uranium ____ ____ ____ ____

9

Read the words in sentences

1. Pots of bright red <u>geraniums</u> lined the steps.

2. We need <u>uranium</u> ore for bombs and medical tools such as x-rays.

3. Her high fever had brought on <u>delirium</u>, and she spoke wildly.

ia

Combine the syllables into whole words and read them.

> In these 8 words, you will make all three sounds of *er*.

1. bac ter i a   *bacteria*
2. im per i al   _____
3. caf e ter i a   _____
4. per en ni al   _____

5. her ni a   _____
6. ser i al   _____
7. ma ter i al   _____
8. in ter me di ate   _____

Read the words in sentences.

1. They need new <u>material</u> for curtains in the <u>cafeteria</u>.

2. A bulging out of the intestine is called a <u>hernia</u>.

3. If you miss one part of a <u>serial</u> on TV, you feel lost with the next one.

4. Our bodies fight off many kinds of <u>bacteria</u> every day.

5. An <u>imperial</u> gallon in Canada is larger than our gallon.

6. Most lilies are <u>perennial</u>; they come up every year.

7. My <u>intermediate</u>-size car uses less gas than a Cadillac.

Dictionary Marks and Less-Common Words

---

her (hur)	**here** (hir)
bird (burd)	**very** (ver′ ē)
fur (fur)	**spirit** (spir′ it)
jury (joor′ ē)*	

While the dictionary shows differences between each of these sounds, some are really very close. You just need to be aware of how a dictionary respells words. Also, dictionaries may differ from one another in how they represent different vowel sounds. To see how common key words are marked, check the page bottom of your dictionary (or look in the front of the book). Getting acquainted with one dictionary is the best way.

---

*In some **ur** words, the **u** sound, not **ur**, is respelled: **jury** (joor′ ē) and **during** (door′ing). This respelling you know from the **u** chapter in *Book One*.

---

1. Learning the Markings with Words You Know

Write the word after the respelling. Try to spell the word without looking at the list.

berry	furry	fury	jerk	learn
miracle	nerve	shirt	sincere	there

1. shurt _____shirt_____
2. ber′ ē _____
3. lurn _____
4. ther _____
5. mir′ ə k′l _____

6. nurv _____
7. jurk _____
8. fur′ ē _____
9. fyoor′ ē _____
10. sin sir′ _____

11

2. Writing Less-Common Words

Write the words in the blanks.

> bursitis   cherish   dexterity   federal   heritage
> infirm   mural   reverence   sterile   vermin

1. We must _____ (cher′ ish) and care for our old, _____ (in fʉrm′) people in nursing homes.

2. She used _____ (ster′ ′l) soil so that bugs and other _____ (vʉr′ min) couldn't kill the potted plants.

3. The flag is part of our _____ (her′ ət ij), and most people have a feeling of _____ (rev′ ər əns) when they see it.

4. My surgeon had _____ (bər sī′ təs) in his shoulder, and his fingers had lost their _____ (dek ster′ ə tē).

5. The _____ (fed′ ər əl) government is in Washington, DC.

6. He used the whole wall to paint a brightly colored _____ (myoor′ əl).

Write the words after the respellings.

> affirmative   conspiracy   curriculum   generic   hibernate
> terminate   turbulent   venereal   vertical   virile

1. vir′ əl   _____
2. hī′ bər nāt′   _____
3. və nir′ ē əl   _____
4. kə rik′ yə ləm   _____
5. kən spir′ ə sē   _____

6. tʉr′ byə lənt   _____
7. jə ner′ ik   _____
8. vʉr′ ti k'l   _____
9. tʉr′ mə nāt′   _____
10. ə fʉr′ mə tiv   _____

Read the words in sentences.

1. The company must act in a more <u>affirmative</u> way in hiring women.

2. Some people think there was a <u>conspiracy</u> to kill President Kennedy, to <u>terminate</u> him, as the gangsters would say.

12

3. American history is in the <u>curriculum</u> of almost every school level.

4. The drugs that can control <u>venereal</u> disease may be available in the less expensive, <u>generic</u> form.

5. Our tenth president had fifteen children; he was a <u>virile</u> man.

6. War stirs people up and creates <u>turbulent</u> times.

7. Animals that <u>hibernate</u> in the cold months do not need food at that time.

8. Bertha drew a <u>vertical</u> line from the top of the wall to the ground.

3. Silent Letters

> You have already been handling *ier* words in which a vowel is silent: **pier** (pir). In **weird** (wird) and in **weir** (wir), a small dam, there is a silent vowel.

Mark out the silent consonants *h, p, w*.

1. Pittsburgh
2. gherkin
3. shepherd
4. raspberry
5. answer
6. rhinoceros
7. cirrhosis
8. Esther

In the following common words, *a* is a silent vowel, and *er* (as in **her**) is the sound: **learn, yearn, earn, Earl, early, earnest, pearl, hearse, rehearse, search, heard**.

Read some of these words in sentences.

1. The <u>shepherds</u> <u>searched</u> for the lost lambs.

2. Ernest drank too much beer and got <u>cirrhosis</u> of the liver.

3. The little <u>gherkin</u> pickles are made in <u>Pittsburgh</u>.

4. <u>Esther</u>, the <u>weird</u>-looking <u>rhinoceros</u>, has a very big horn on her nose.

5. The <u>hearse</u> at the funeral home is a <u>raspberry</u> color with a <u>pearl</u> gray top.

13

4. Out-of-Pattern and Other Confusing Words

☆ In a few words, *er, ir,* and *ur* are split.

- **erase** (e rase)

- **erupt** (e rupt)

- **serene** (se rene)

- **Peru** (Pe ru)

- **pirate** (pi rate)

- **virus** (vi rus)

- **iron** (i ron)

- **siren** (si ren)

- **Irish** (I rish), and a few more.

☆ In some words, *de* is a prefix, **derail** (de rail), and separated from *r*.

☆ In **bury** (ber′ ē) and **burial** (ber′ ē əl), *ur* has the *er* (as in **very**) sound.

☆ Unlike the other *ery* words, the sound in **cemetery** and **monastery** is that of *er* as in **very**.

☆ There are two meanings and two ways of saying **tear**

"Don't **tear** the paper."   "I saw a **tear** on her cheek."

Little Words in Longer Words

1.

Write on a piece of paper the little words in the longer words. Do not include *I*, *an*, or *a*.

1. personality
2. superintendent
3. permafrost
4. concurrent
5. thermometer
6. impersonate
7. infirmity
8. exasperate
9. terminal
10. exterminate

2.

Write on a piece of paper the little words in place and family names.

1. Birmingham
2. Frankfurt
3. Amsterdam
4. Churchill
5. Burgundy
6. Durango
7. Germany
8. Hamburg

"How Do You Say Your Name?"

Names with *er* often make you wonder how to say them, but you develop a sense of what the sound probably is by listening to similar names and by using famous names as models.

Read the famous names that have the two *er* sounds.

President Jefferson

Billy Herman

General Sheridan

George Ferris

Anthony Perkins

Irving Berlin

Don Everly

Bo Derek

Admiral Perry

Handling *er*, *ir*, and *ur* Words . . . Lightly

Informal Words

Some words we've made up have an amusing ring to them. <u>Circle the more informal word in each pair.</u>

1. topsy-turvy—upside down
2. mean trickery—skullduggery
3. fussy—persnickety
4. a twerp—a silly person
5. brave—nervy

6. a dull person—a nerd
7. folderol—nonsense
8. an uproar—hurly-burly
9. gurgle—make a bubbling sound
10. a fool—a jerk

Places or Brands?

All of the following are names of products or places, some of them rather uncommon. <u>Circle the 15 names of places (little towns, cities, states, or countries).</u>

New Jersey	Pertussin	Duracell	Burnt Ranch
Purr-tenders	Zerex	Skunk's Misery	Vermont
Poverty Hill	Gerber	Jerkey Treats	Prosperity
Terminix	Bull Durham	Germany	Thermofil
Perseverance	Deliverance	Burden	Aspercreme
Pittsburgh	Merrymeeting	Efferdent	Virgin
Allergin	Bufferin	Liberia	Siberia

Medical Words

Some words a doctor is not likely to use in his line of work. <u>Cross out the 7 words that have little or nothing to do with health and medicine.</u>

allergy	surgery	tuberculosis	urine
injury	currency	maternity	energy
bursitis	thermometer	nerves	federal
internist	therapy	bacteria	earthquake
mermaid	cirrhosis	merchandise	memory
tabernacle	hernia	aspirin	Terence

"Paid for by Our Tax Dollars?"

<u>Circle any of the following that are **not** paid for by tax dollars—local, county, state, or federal.</u>

Public health nursing	Everglades Park	Sheraton Hotels
Superior Township Hall	U.S. Dept. of Interior	Fertilizer plants
Kentucky Derby race track	Pillsbury Mills	Xerox Company
Burlington Industries	Ferrell Country Geriatric Health Service	Murder Burger
University of Vermont	U.S. Dept. of Commerce	Pittsburgh Pirates
U.S. Navy Reserves	Hurricane warnings	Sheriff patrol
Cherokee Indian Reserve	New Jersey prisons	Michigan Lottery

What's New?

In the early days of the United States, life was very different in some ways from life today. In other ways, things haven't changed a great deal. Check the 9 things that the early Americans would **not** have done.

1. __ eaten at a cafeteria
2. __ attended church services
3. __ used an answering service
4. __ irritated each other
5. __ dropped a camera
6. __ sent children to Head Start or other nursery schools
7. __ sat in a bus terminal
8. __ gone to government ceremonies
9. __ heard a sermon
10. __ listened to the "Blue Murder" group
11. __ eaten frozen yogurt
12. __ worried about an energy crisis
13. __ bought batteries for toys
14. __ killed vermin in their homes

Choosing a Product Name

An advertising company works hard at finding the right name to appeal to customers. Circle the words that would make you want to buy perfume.

Above Average	Surrender	Burden
Bolero	Emerald	Turkey Wing
Different Smell	Vera	On the Terrace
Misery Loves Company	Dark Amber	Assertive Woman

18

Chapter 2
ar and *or*

ar as in **car** (kär)　　*ar* as in **carry** (kar′ē)

ar as in **war** (wôr)

or as in **corn** (kôrn)　　*or* as in **word** (wυrd)

Sound and Spelling

1. The Sounds of *ar* as in **car, carry,** and **war.**

The Sound of *ar* as in **car.**

This is the most common sound of *ar*. There is a slight difference in the way this sound is made, depending on what part of the country you grew up in.

Write the words that have the same vowel sound and the same consonant ending as the numbered word.

bark　　card　　harp　　lard　　mark　　spark　　yard

1. hard _____ _____ _____

2. dark _____ _____ _____

3. sharp _____

19

The Sound of *ar* as in **care**

> This is the same sound you hear in **bear, pear, wear, swear,** in **very, there,** and in **air, fair, pair**.

> Not everyone says and hears the sounds of *ar* in **carry** and **care** the same way. They are so close they will be treated as the same sound here.

Read the words and listen to the sound of *ar* as in care and carry.

bare, blare, dare, fare, marry, rare, scare, share, spare

The Sound of *ar* as in **war.**

If *ar* follows *w, wh,* or *qu,* the sound you hear is *or,* in most words. There are not many, and most of them are common words.

Read the words and listen to the sound of *ar* as in war.

war, warn, warm, ward, wart, quart, and quarrel

Read sentences with some of these words and others, all with *ar* sounds.

1. The lard for the pie crust will melt in this warm weather.

2. Had I sailed on the ark, the tigers would have scared me at mealtimes.

3. A lark sang in a tree as we fished for carp; we didn't snare one fish.

4. I must warn you that leaving the lumber out on the wharf to be shipped may cause it to warp.

5. Not being interested in clothes, she wore any old garb.

6. Rose quartz, not a rare stone, has a lovely, warm color.

20

Longer, Common Words with *ar*

Write in *ar* and read the words. You will be saying all of the *ar* sounds.

1. c __ __ ton
2. n __ __ row
3. h __ __ vest
4. qu __ __ rel

5. b __ __ becue
6. rad __ __
7. b __ __ gain
8. w __ __ rant

9. p __ __ ent
10. g __ __ lic
11. p __ __ rot
12. w __ __ drobe

13. welf __ __ e
14. b __ __ ren
15. __ __ tery
16. g __ __ ment

2. The Sounds of *or* as in **corn** and in **word**

or as in **corn**

Write the words that have the same vowel sound and the same consonant ending as the numbered word.

born   cork   dorm   pork   stork   storm   thorn   torn

1. corn   _____, _____, _____
2. form   _____, _____
3. fork   _____, _____, _____

or as in **word**

If *or* follows *w*, the sound you hear, in most words, is *ur* as in **hurt**. There are very few of these words and most of them are common.

Read the words and listen to the sound of *or* as in word.

work, world, worm, worry, worse, worst, worth

Read sentences with some of these words, and others with the *or* sounds.

1. I heard the <u>horses</u> <u>snort</u> and whinny all during the <u>storm</u>.

2. The blacksmith's <u>forge</u> is the <u>worst</u> place to <u>work</u> in hot weather.

3. We found many <u>worms</u> under a <u>cord</u> of wood in back of the <u>fort</u>.

4. Where in the <u>world</u> did he get that <u>torn</u> and <u>worn</u> shirt?

5. The <u>story</u> of <u>storks</u> carrying babies is <u>worse</u> than the Easter bunny tale.

Longer, Common Words with *or*

Write in *or* and read the words. You will be saying both sounds of *or*.

1. f __ __ est
2. p __ __ ter
3. w __ __ thy

4. h __ __ net
5. w __ __ ship
6. t __ __ nado

7. m __ __ al
8. res __ __ t
9. w __ __ kshop

10. w __ __ thwhile
11. fl __ __ ist
12. w __ __ ldwide

3. Spelling *ar* and *or* Words

As with *r* vowel words in the last chapter, you need to use the dictionary often when spelling *ar* and *or* words you don't use every day.

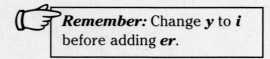 ***Remember:*** Change *y* to *i* before adding *er*.

Write the words and add *er*.

1. carry _____
2. dark _____
3. worthy _____

4. stormy _____
5. scary _____
6. form _____

Write the words and add *s* or *es*.

☞ ***Remember:*** Add *es*, not *s*, to words ending in *ch*. Change *y* to *i* in the words before adding *es* and *age*.

1. worry _____
2. march _____
3. star _____
4. story _____

5. garter _____
6. marble _____
7. marry _____
8. porch _____

Write the word and add *age*.

1. marry _____   2. carry _____

Syllables and Accents

1. Writing Words in Syllables

Write the syllables in the blanks and put in the main accent marks.

1. important   _____ _____ _____
2. marshmallow   _____ _____ _____
3. supportive   _____ _____ _____
4. argument   _____ _____ _____
5. worsening   _____ _____ _____
6. horrible   _____ _____ _____
7. embarrass   _____ _____ _____
8. warranty   _____ _____ _____
9. transparent   _____ _____ _____
10. correspond   _____ _____ _____
11. participate   _____ _____ _____ _____
12. charitable   _____ _____ _____ _____

2. *ar* and *or* Suffixes/Endings

ar as in **beggar** or **cellar** and *or* as in **doctor** or **victor**

These are common suffixes/endings, often so woven into the words that they can't be dropped from the word. They have the schwa sound, and therefore they sound the same. You must remember which is which or go to the dictionary.

ary as in **voluntary** and ***ory*** as in **directory**

> There are two syllables in both **ary** and **ory**.

Write the words in syllables in the lists. Put in the main accent mark.

> Don't forget the first ***r*** in **library**.

| accessory | anniversary | customary | introductory | lavatory |
| library | necessary | satisfactory | secretary | territory |

ary   ***ory***

_____   _____

_____   _____

_____   _____

_____   _____

3. Word Building

Put a slash between the syllables. Put in the main accent marks and read the words and sentences.

1. **order**   **orderly**   **disorder**   **disorderly**   **disorderliness**

   He liked order. His desk was very orderly. The disorder of his friend's room bothered him. He couldn't have her arrested for disorderly conduct. He simply had to put up with her disorderliness.

2. **part**   **participate**   **participant**   **participating**

   We took part in the holiday. Will you participate in the game? Yes, I will be a participant in your game. I will be participating like a winner.

24

3. argue   arguing   argument   argumentative

Let's not <u>argue</u> about it. They are always <u>arguing</u>. Who can settle the <u>argument</u>? These people are so <u>argumentative</u>!

4. normal   normally   abnormal   normalize   abnormality

He is a <u>normal</u> child. <u>Normally</u>, I leave late. Snow in October is <u>abnormal</u> weather. The United States will try to <u>normalize</u> relations with Cuba. He needed help because of an <u>abnormality</u> of the spine.

4. Split Vowels

ia

Put a slash between the syllables and then write the words in the blanks.

his/tor/ian   janitorial   librarian   malaria
memorial   senatorial   variance   vegetarian

1. She loves books and wants to be a _____.
2. Carol eats no fish, chicken, or other meat; she is a _____.
3. We sadly attended the _____ service at the church.
4. You must be strong to do some kinds of _____ work.
5. High fever and chills are part of the misery of _____.
6. Not every _____ can write lively, readable history.
7. The man was a _____ aid to Senator Darren.
8. There is a big _____ between my paycheck and yours.

iu, ea, eo

Combine the syllables into whole words.

1. a quar i um   _____
2. plan e tar i um   _____
3. cre ma tor i um   _____
4. san i tar i um   _____
5. Kor e a   _____
6. de o dor ant   _____
7. ar e a   _____

Read these words in sentences.

1. The goldfish in my aquarium are of the ordinary kind.

2. Fewer people have tuberculosis, so the sanitarium now has closed.

3. Instead of being buried, the body was taken to the crematorium.

4. It was raining, so we went to the planetarium to study the stars.

5. Korea, a country next to China, is divided into two parts; one area is controlled by a Communist government.

Dictionary Marks and Less-Common Words

car (kär)
care (ker)
carry (kar′ ē)
quart (kwôrt)
war (wôr)
corn (kôrn)
word (wurd)

The dictionary respells the sound of *ar* as in **care** and **parent** the way it respells *er* in **very** (ver′ē): **care** (ker), **parent** (per′ ənt). Many of us don't hear a difference in these *ar* sounds. All that matters here is understanding the dictionary respellings. Both *ar* and *or* can be a schwa.

1. Learning the Markings with Words You Know

Write the word after the respelling. Try to spell the words without looking at the list.

bar	beggar	blare	born
doctor	square	ward	worst

1. bär _____

2. bôrn _____

3. wôrd _____

4. skwer _____

5. wurst _____

6. dok′ tər _____

7. beg′ ər _____

8. bler _____

2. Writing Less-Common Words

Write the words after the respellings.

arbitrator	carcinogen	carnage	garnishee
horizon	parallel	porcelain	torrent

1. pôr′ s'l in _____

2. gär′ nə shē′ _____

3. par′ ə lel′ _____

4. kär′ nij _____

5. kär sin′ ə jən _____

6. är′ bə trā′ tər _____

7. hə rī′ z'n _____

8. tôr′ ənt _____

Read these words in sentences.

1. She broke her fine <u>porcelain</u> teacups.

2. The <u>carnage</u> of the animals on the highways over a holiday is shocking.

3. A <u>torrent</u> of rain and hail made us pull over to the side for awhile.

4. The <u>horizon</u> is where the sky appears to meet the earth.

5. Courts may <u>garnishee</u> wages if debts aren't paid.

6. The slats of a blind form <u>parallel</u> lines, each one equally distant from the other.

7. Any substance that might cause cancer is a <u>carcinogen</u>.

8. To get an agreement, the company and workers called in an <u>arbitrator</u>.

Write the words in the blanks.

Arabic	cardiogram	cartilage	commissary	dormant
marinade	mortality	ordinance	paralegal	parliament

1. The doctor ordered a _____ (kär′ dē ə gram′) done after her heart attack.

2. Food in the army _____ (kom′ ə ser′ ē) is cheaper than in other stores.

3. During the winter, plants lie _____ (dôr′ mənt) until spring.

4. Canada doesn't have a Congress; it has a _____ (pär′ lə mənt).

5. The parking _____ (ôr′ d'n əns) was approved by the mayor.

6. She took _____ (par′ ə lē′ gəl) training so she could be a lawyer's assistant at Legal Aid.

7. The stiff part of the ear is called _____ (kärt′ 'l ij).

8. The meat was in a _____ (mar′ ə nād′) of oil, vinegar, and spices.

9. People speak _____ (ar′ ə bik) in many lands, not just in Arabia.

10. The _____ (môr tal′ ə tē) numbers after the hurricane were very high.

3. Silent Letters

Silent *h, g, u*

Write the words in the lists.

arraign	Deborah	guarantee	guardian	
guitar	honor	morgue	rhubarb	sorghum

Silent *h*	Silent *g*	Silent *u*
_____	_____	_____
_____		_____
_____		_____
_____		

Other Silent-Letter Words

Put a slash through the silent letter and read the word.

1. jeopardy (jep′ ər dē)

2. parfait (pär fā′)

3. corps (kôr)

4. sword (sôrd)

5. czar or tsar (zär)

6. mortgage (môr′ gij)

7. psoriasis (sə rī′ ə sis)

8. corpuscle (kôr′ pəs ′l)

Read some of these words with silent letters in sentences.

1. Children playing with guns and <u>swords</u> put others in <u>jeopardy</u>.

2. The drug <u>czar</u> had a <u>corps</u> of trained men to protect him.

3. People suffering from <u>psoriasis</u> have scaly, reddish skin patches.

4. The ice cream <u>parfait</u> is a French food, but <u>sorghum</u> molasses is American.

5. White <u>corpuscles</u> in the blood help fight off some germs.

6. The court will formally <u>arraign</u> the accused kidnapper.

7. A bank president tries not to approve any bad <u>mortgages</u> for houses.

4. Out-of-Pattern and Other Confusing Words

☆ **attorney:** The *or* sounds like *ur* (ə tur′ nē), even in the accented syllable.

☆ **worn** and **sworn:** The *w* does not turn *or* into an *er* sound.

☆ **Arkansas:** The last syllable sounds like **saw**.

You hear *ar* as in **car**, not *er*, in **sergeant** (sär′ jənt).

Little Words in Longer Words

1.

Write on a piece of paper the little words in longer words.

1. harmony
2. partisan
3. artillery
4. artichoke
5. formulate
6. parsonage
7. misdemeanor
8. articulate
9. asparagus
10. importance

2.

Write on a piece of paper the little words in names of places.

1. Carbondale
2. Normandy
3. Mamaroneck
4. Madagascar
5. Delaware
6. Orlando
7. Formosa
8. Antarctic
9. Leavenworth

"How Do You Say Your Name?"

Names with *ar* often leave you wondering how to say them. If there is a double *r*, the sound may be *ar*, as in **carry**, but not always. You often have to ask the person how to say the name.

Read the names and try out the sounds of *ar*.

Larson	Garrison	Garvey	Paret
Harper	Harrell	Agar	Lombardi
Carroll	Armstrong	Barnett	Maris
Aaron	Parson	Carew	Garrett
Harrington	Cardoza	Gazzaro	Arnold

Handling *ar* and *or* Words . . . Lightly

Suitable Words

In writing a complaint letter, one needs to be clear, polite, and firm. <u>Circle the words that</u> <u>may **not** be suitable to use in a letter of complaint.</u>

smarty-pants	similar	embarrass	blarney
worry-wart	pardonable	dorky	particularly
worthwhile	ignorant	normal	moron
correspondence	attorney	varmint	stubborn
malarky	participate	satisfactory	lardhead
inventory	subnormal	originally	garbage

Jobs: Indoor or Outdoor?

<u>Circle the 5 jobs that are performed mainly outdoors.</u>

Ozarks forest ranger	marble quarry foreman
reformatory guard	paralegal aid at Legal Services
quartet singing at Paradise Club	catching sharks for the aquarium
Antarctic explorer	coroner at morgue and crematorium
collecting garbage and refuse	teaching a correspondence course
orderly at mental sanitorium	secretary for an attorney
laboratory helper	dormitory cook

A Little Too Clever?

Some of the following names of businesses are too clever because you can't tell what kind of product or service you would be getting just by looking at the name. <u>Check the ones that leave you wondering.</u>

Marvel	The Orange Crate	Amazing Grace for Vegetarians
The March Hair	Head Quarters	Aardvark Pest Control
Arrow Shirt Shop	Great Performances	Worn Out West
Pillar to Post	The Storage Bin	Starvin' Marvin
Chores Unlimited	Canine Kindergarten	Commissary Kitchen
Party Lines	Old Horizons	Adorable Escort Service

Magazines

<u>Circle the 11 names of magazines, weekly or monthly.</u>

Car and Driver	Inside Sports	Arctic Plants
Ignorance	Motor Trends	Organic Gardening
Drixornal and Colds	Parents	Tony Orlando's Life
Harper's	Pardonable Sin	Forum
Wells Fargo Robberies	New York Magazine	Vegetarian Times
Boring Times	Sports Illustrated	Parenting

Names and Nicknames

States and cities, like people, often have nicknames. Circle the nicknames that people have given to American places.

Hell's Forty Acres   Tarheel   Corncracker   Cornhusker

Florida   Colorado   Cornopolis   Buzzard

Land of Opportunity   Porkopolis   North Carolina   Port Arthur

Port of Missing Men   Charleston   Bismarck   Arizona

Hornet's Nest   Norman   Arkansas   Oregon

Land of Lizard   Wharton   Warren   Saratoga

Heart of Dixie   Garden   Peace Garden   Lone Star

Gifts

Check the gifts you think someone would like to get.

carrot cake   coral beads   acorns   a garbage bag

a corduroy purse   a scarf   a big carton   oxford shoes

a formal dress   a parakeet   a bullhorn   box of caramels

can of varnish   marble table   carpet tacks   a corset

Morocco leather box   jar of marmalade   garden hose   sparklers

bed comforter   carfare   a guitar   lard

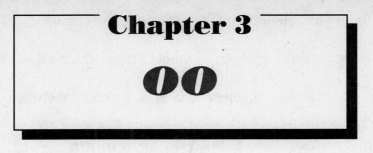

Chapter 3
OO

oo as in **moon** (mo͞on)   *oo* as in **book** (book)

Sound and Spelling

1. The Sound of *oo* as in **moon**

oo as in **moon** is the same sound you heard in **lose** (lo͞oz), **shoe** (sho͞o), and **womb** (wo͞om) in the *o* and in the *u* chapters of *Book 1*.

Write the words that have the same vowel sound and the same consonant ending as the numbered word.

boom	brood	broom	goose	loot	mood
moose	noose	stoop	swoop	toot	troop

1. food _____ _____

2. loop _____ _____ _____

3. boot _____ _____

4. loose _____ _____ _____

5. room _____ _____

Read sentences with some of these words and others with *oo*.

1. The <u>zoom</u> lens of the camera is used for close-ups.

2. He would <u>brood</u> over things he couldn't change and get into a bad <u>mood</u>.

3. The farmer put a <u>noose</u> around the neck of the <u>goose</u>.

35

4. I heard a great <u>boom</u> and thought my day of <u>doom</u> had come.

5. He said he would <u>scoot</u> down and get something to <u>soothe</u> his nerves.

6. A <u>troop</u> of boys would <u>swoop</u> into a street and clean up all the trash.

Longer, Common Words with *oo* as in **moon**

Write in *oo* and read the words.

1. shamp __ __	**5.** racc __ __ n	**9.** h __ __ ray	**13.** whiskbr __ __ m
2. r __ __ ster	**6.** n __ __ dle	**10.** f __ __ lpr __ __ f	**14.** t __ __ lbox
3. mushr __ __ m	**7.** p __ __ dle	**11.** teasp __ __ n	**15.** rustpr __ __ f
4. t __ __ thpaste	**8.** sc __ __ ter	**12.** whirlp __ __ l	**16.** l __ __ phole

2. The Sound of *oo* as in **book**

> *oo* as in **book** is the same sound
> you heard in **pull** (pool) and **push**
> (poosh) in the *u* chapter of *Book 1*.

Write the words that have the same vowel sound and the same consonant ending as the numbered words.

brook	cook	crook	hook	shook	stood	took	wood

1. good _____ _____

2. book _____ _____ _____ _____ _____

_____

Longer, Common Words with *oo* as in **book**

Write in *oo* and read the words.

1. hardw __ __ d	**4.** handb __ __ k	**7.** b __ __ kkeeper	**10.** baref __ __ t
2. c __ __ kie	**5.** fishh __ __ k	**8.** underst __ __ d	**11.** c __ __ kb __ __ k
3. f __ __ thold	**6.** motherh __ __ d	**9.** w __ __ dchuck	**12.** g __ __ dl __ __ king

36

3. Spelling *oo* Words

Write the words and add *ing*, *ed*, and *er*.

Do not double the final letter in *oo* words. When adding endings, *oo* words are treated like long-vowel words (which they are not).

1. cook   _____, _____, _____

2. room   _____, _____, _____

3. loot   _____, _____, _____

4. shampoo   _____, _____, _____

☞ **Remember:** Change *y* to *i*.

Write the words and add *er* and *est*.

1. moody   _____   _____

2. gloomy   _____   _____

3. roomy   _____   _____

4. spooky   _____   _____

5. bloody   _____   _____

Syllables and Accents

1. Writing Words in Syllables

Write the words in syllables and put in the main accent mark.

1. honeymoon   _____ _____ _____

2. cookery   _____ _____ _____

3. brotherhood   _____ _____ _____

4. crookedness   _____ _____ _____

5. loosening   _____ _____ _____

6. foolishness   _____ _____ _____

7. foolhardy _____ _____ _____

8. soothingly _____ _____ _____

Dictionary Marks and Less-Common Words

---

moon (mo͞on) **book** (book)

The only difference in the respelling is a line over the **oo** (as in **moon**). The schwa does not replace **oo**.

1. Writing Less-Common Words

Write the word after the respelling.

boomerang	caboose	cartoon	cocoon	festoon
hoodwink	lagoon	macaroon	platoon	taboo

1. kə bo͞os′ _____

2. lə go͞on′ _____

3. plə to͞on′ _____

4. fes to͞on′ _____

5. mak′ ə ro͞on′ _____

6. tə bo͞o′ _____

7. kə ko͞on′ _____

8. kär to͞on′ _____

9. bo͞om′ ə raŋ′ _____

10. hood′ wiŋk′ _____

Read these words in sentences.

1. An army <u>platoon</u> waded across the <u>lagoon</u>, holding the guns high.

2. A <u>boomerang</u> will return to you if you throw it right.

3. We can <u>festoon</u> lights across the front porch for the party.

4. The butterfly came out of the <u>cocoon</u> and let its wings dry.

5. In that family, it was strictly <u>taboo</u> to talk back to the parents.

6. Saturday morning the children look at one <u>cartoon</u> after another.

38

7. The brakeman rides in the <u>caboose</u>, the last car of the train.

8. A coconut <u>macaroon</u> is a good cookie if it is made right.

9. Don't let a salesman <u>hoodwink</u> you into buying useless things.

2. Out-of-Pattern and Other Confusing Words

☆ You hear the short **u** sound in **flood** (flud) and **blood** (blud).

☆ In **floor** (flôr) and **door** (dôr), you hear the **or** sound.

☆ The **s** in **choose** has a **z** sound, but not in **goose, loose**, or **moose**.

☆ The following words have more than one way of saying them depending on where you grew up:

  - **roof** (roof or rōof)

  - **hoof** (hoof or hōof)

  - **soot** (soot or sōot)

  - **root** (root or rōot)

☆ In a very few words, **oo** must be split into separate syllables:

  - **cooperate** (kō op′ ə rāt′)

  - **coop**, the shortened word, (kō′ op)

  - **coordinate** (kō ôr′ də nāt′)

There are only a few more.

Little Words in Longer Words

Write on a piece of paper the little words in the place names.

1. Rangoon
2. Kalamazoo
3. Liverpool
4. Brookhaven
5. Woonsocket
6. Bloomington
7. Chattahoochee
8. Bloomsburg
9. Mattoon

''How Do You Say Your Name?''

All of the following are family names. They are names people often get teased about. You might need to ask how to spell them.

Read the names and notice the ones that sound like common words, even though the spelling may not be the same.

Woods	Brooks	Yomtoob	Hoover
Shook	Crooks	Yoo	Boozer
Wooley	Coonley	Hooley	Koop
Tooms	Hooten	Soos	Hooper

Handling *oo* Words . . . Lightly

Funny-Sounding Words

We have made up many informal words with the **oo** sounds. Play titles using **oo** nonsense words are clearly comedies: "Kitchy-Koo," "Toot-Toot!," "Whoop-De-Doo," "Ballyhoo," "Hip! Hip! Hooray!," and "Tootsie."

Silly talk is a lot of hooey or gobbledygook. You say "Oops!" when you make a booboo. People on TV call a mistake a blooper. If you can't name something, you call it a doodad, a doohickey, or, if it's wet, goop. Making a big show of something is ballyhoo or hoopla. A woman may be called a floozy for making googoo eyes at a man. Someone who doesn't do the right thing is a goof-off or a big galloot or a yahoo. If you trick people you bamboozle or hoodwink them. It wasn't very groovy of you to pull a switcheroo on them. Were you in cahoots with the devil? When you behave in a silly way, you are seen as goofy, kooky, or loony. They say you are a booby from the boondocks.

If you drink too much booze or hooch, you become woozy. You may even lose your moola and have to mooch off someone. Your friends get into a flapdoodle about it and raise a big hullabaloo. They say that this tomfoolery has to stop and if it doesn't, toodle-oo to you. They want nothing to do with the whole kit-and-caboodle. You end up with a doozy of a hangover and may play hooky from your job. You worry about someone using voodoo on you. But when you quit drinking, your friends say, "Goody-goody! Hooray for you! Whoopee!"

Addresses or Movie Titles

Circle the 9 place names you might see as someone's address on an envelope.

Kalamazoo, MI	**The Blue Lagoon**	**Spooner**
The Appaloosa	**Yazoo City, MS**	**Dr. Doolittle**
Waterloo Bridge	**Oskaloosa, IA**	**Secret of the Ooze**
Baraboo, WI	**Blood and Sand**	**Woonsocket, RI**
Chattanooga, TN	**Wooster, OH**	**Platoon**
Yankee Doodle	**Tuscaloosa, AL**	**Goodnight, TX**

Name the Business

Circle a name you might choose for each of the following businesses.

Children's toys, clothing

Baby Boom

Sweet Zoo

Dottie Doolittle

The Balloon Man

Restaurant

Standing Room Only

Fools Rush Inn

Snooty Fox

Chick and Coop

The Boondocks

Woodshed Eatery

Bar and grill

Wahoo Bar & Grill

Mr. Flood's Party

Wooden Nickel

The Men's Room

Hoodoo Bar & Grill

Bloody Mary's

Flowers, gifts

Goosebumps

Nooks 'N Granny

Hullaballoons

Business Is Blooming

Pets and pet care

Pamper Poodle

Groom and Board

The Poodle Cut

Yankee Doodle Pets

Animals?

Circle the names of 12 animals.

raccoon	kangaroo	bookworm	boondocks
rooster	nincompoop	moose	stool-pigeon
bugaboo	voodoo	poodle	booby hatch
gooseberry	buckaroo	baboon	woodchuck
boomerang	cockatoo	hoodlum	mongoose
cuckoo	boondoggle	rook	loon

Chapter 4
oi and *oy*

oi as in **oil** (oil)   *oy* as in **boy** (boi)

io as in **lion** (lī ən)

Sound and Spelling

1. The Sound of *oi* as in **oil** and *oy* as in **boy**

These two pairs of vowels have the same sound.

Write the words that have the same vowel and the same consonant ending as the numbered word.

foil   hoist   joint   Joyce   Lloyd   Roy   toy   voice

1. moist _____   **4.** void _____

2. point _____   **5.** boil _____

3. boy _____ _____   **6.** choice _____ _____

Read sentences with some of these words and others with *oi* and *oy*.

1. Lloyd put the car up on a hoist to work on it.

2. Joyce had her knee joint replaced.

3. The carpenter fixed the rotten floor joists.

4. The soy plant has beans.

5. Roy made coins out of aluminum foil.

6. The groin is where the legs join the rest of the body.

Longer, Common Words with *oi*

Write in *oi* and read the words.

1. tinf __ __ l

2. t __ __ let

3. p __ __ son

4. inv __ __ ce

5. app __ __ nt

6. sirl __ __ n

7. g __ __ ter

8. rec __ __ l

9. av __ __ d

10. rej __ __ ce

11. tenderl __ __ n

12. n __ __ sy

Longer, Common Words with *oy*

Write in *oy* and read the words.

1. ann __ __

2. destr __ __

3. empl __ __

4. enj __ __

5. l __ __ al

6. r __ __ al

7. __ __ ster

8. s __ __ bean

9. v __ __ age

10. ah __ __

11. b __ __ hood

12. b __ __ cott

2. Spelling *oi* and *oy* Words

> In spelling these pairs of vowels, you may have to look up *oi* and then, perhaps, *oy*. The same holds true of finding names in the telephone book.

Write the words and add *ing*, *ed*, and *er*.

As in *oo* words, you do not double the final letter in *oi* and *oy* words when you add an ending.

1. boil _____, _____, _____

2. point _____, _____, _____

3. destroy _____, _____, _____

Syllables and Accents

1. Writing Words in Syllables

Write the words in syllables and put in the main accent mark.

1. loyally   _____ _____ _____
2. ointment   _____ _____
3. enjoyable   _____ _____ _____ _____
4. unenjoyable   _____ _____ _____ _____ _____
5. corduroy   _____ _____ _____
6. noiselessly   _____ _____ _____
7. disappointment   _____ _____ _____ _____
8. embroidery   _____ _____ _____ _____

2. Word Building

Mark the syllables with slashes and put in the main accent. Read the sentences.

1. **employ**   **employee**   **employer**   **employment**   **employable**

   When will they employ more people? The employer told her employee to go home. Even highly employable people were looking for employment daily.

2. **annoy**   **annoying**   **annoyance**

   Don't annoy me with silly questions. That music is so annoying. Tapping on the back of my chair is an annoyance.

3. **avoid**   **avoidance**   **avoidable**   **unavoidable**

   He will avoid meeting me on the street. His avoidance of me hurt my feelings. On a clear, dry road, the accident was avoidable. Laying off workers was unavoidable in bad times.

3. Split-Vowel Words

io: When *i* comes before *o*, the sound is not *oi* as in **oil**. The sounds of *i* and *o* (or the schwa) are heard separately.

Mark the words in syllables and then write them in the blanks.

an|ti|bi|ot|ic   idiot   lion   Lionel   Ohio

patio   pioneers   radio   violate   violin

1. Ask _____ to please turn down the

_____.

2. He was an _____ to get so close to the fierce

_____.

3. The doctor gave me an _____ for my sore throat.

4. In the 1800's, _____ came to what is now the state

of _____ in covered wagons.

5. As she started to play, a string broke on her

_____.

6. We sat on the brick _____ at the back of his

house.

7. How could he ask a child to _____ the law?

Combine the syllables into a whole word and put in the main accent mark.

1. tap i o ca _____   4. di o cese _____

2. vi o let _____   5. i o dine _____

3. bi ol o gy _____   6. bi op sy _____

Read the words in sentences.

1. We made <u>tapioca</u> pudding.

2. In <u>biology</u> class we studied the human body for months.

46

3. My doctor removed a mole and had a <u>biopsy</u> done to check for cancer.

4. The bishop not only says mass but also oversees a big <u>diocese</u>.

5. In early spring, the <u>violet</u> can be seen blooming everywhere.

6. Putting <u>iodine</u> on a cut hurts and the brown color looks ugly.

Dictionary Marks and Less-Common Words

> **oil** (oil), **boy** (boi)

The dictionary respells *oy* as if it were *oi*.

> Since *oi* and *oy* have the same sound, you may have to look up one and then the other spelling when using the dictionary or the telephone book.

1. Writing Less-Common Words

Write the word after the respelling.

alloy	asteroid	convoy	deploy	exploit
loiter	mastoid	Mongoloid	turquoise	steroid

1. ster′ oid _____

2. mas′ toid _____

3. kon′ voi _____

4. eks ploit′ _____

5. loi′ tər _____

6. dē ploi′ _____

7. tʉr′ koiz _____

8. al′ loi _____

9. as′ tə roid′ _____

10. moŋ′ gə loid′ _____

Read the words in sentences.

1. Taking <u>steroid</u> drugs will develop the body—and destroy it.

2. He was hit right behind the ear, on the <u>mastoid</u> bone.

3. A <u>convoy</u> of destroyers protected the President's ship.

4. The company pays low wages and no benefits; it <u>exploits</u> the workers.

5. Homeless men would <u>loiter</u> in the library on cold days.

6. The navy won't <u>deploy</u> the new ship until it is tested.

7. Her dress was the same <u>turquoise</u> blue as her ring.

8. When metals are mixed, you have an <u>alloy</u>.

9. A small planet near Mars is called an <u>asteroid</u>.

10. The people of China and Japan belong to the <u>Mongoloid</u> race.

2. Silent Letters

Write the words in the blanks and then mark out silent *h, r, t, u*.

buoyant   hemorrhoids   moisten   rheumatoid

1. You must _____ (mois′ 'n) the soil of the plant twice a week.

2. Her grandmother suffered from _____ (roo′ mə toid′) arthritis in her back and joints.

3. If the boat isn't _____ (boi′ ənt), it won't float.

4. The _____ (hem′ ə roids′) were so painful he couldn't sit.

3. Out-of-Pattern and Other Confusing Words

☆ In most words, *oi* is in the accented syllable. This is not the case in **tortoise** (tôr′ təs), a kind of turtle, and **porpoise** (pôr′ pəs), a large sea animal.

☆ In a few words, *oi* is split and does not have the *oi* as in **oil** sound.

- **Lois** (lō′ is), the woman's name
- **heroin** (her′ ə win), the drug
- **heroine** (her′ ə win), the brave woman
- **heroic** (hi rō′ ik), the way brave people act

☆ *co* is a prefix and a separate syllable in **coincidence** (kō in′ sə dəns) meaning accidentally happening at the same time, and **coincide** (kō′ in sīd′), meaning to take up the same place in space.

Little Words in Longer Words

Write the little words on a piece of paper.

1. Hotpoint
2. Sheboygan
3. Livernois
4. Toyota
5. Illinois
6. Boykin
7. Perth Amboy
8. trapezoid

''How Do You Say Your Name?''

Since *oy* and *oi* have the same sound, it is not difficult to say people's names with these pairs of vowels.

Read the famous names and listen to the sounds of *oi* and *oy*.

Bill Boyd

Captain Boycott

Leo Tolstoy

Bill Moyers

William Dubois

Senator Moynihan

Jon Voight

Admiral Poindexter

William Saroyan

General Burgoyne

Edward Hoyle

Arthur Conan Doyle

49

Handling *oi* and *oy* Words . . . Lightly

Medical Words

Cross out the 7 words that have little to do with medicine.

joints	paranoid	adenoids	ointment	hemorrhoids
coins	steroids	embroider	groin	rheumatoid
tinfoil	goiter	polio	biopsy	spoilsport
fibroid	mastoid	bellboy	patriot	broiler

Business Names

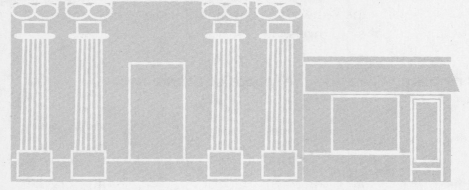

Some business names are chosen to catch the eye of customers. Circle the names of businesses that might be noticed because of the name.

The Sirloin Strip	Bank of Tokyo	The Pet Spoilers
Polaroid Corp.	Owens-Illinois, Inc.	Canine Clip Joint
Curiosity Shop	Killroy Bar & Grill	Toyota Sales
The Hare and Tortoise Running Shop	Tif-Toi Poodle Groomers	American Hoist and Derrick

Words, Good and Bad

Some words carry a bad, or negative, feeling. Others always make one feel good, or positive. Write **b** (for "bad") or **g** (for "good") before the words.

____ loyal	____ violated	____ disappointed
____ unemployed	____ heroic	____ joyful
____ rejoice	____ idiotic	____ spoiled
____ annoying	____ exploited	____ rheumatoid
____ poisoned	____ noisy	____ noiseless
____ loitering	____ turmoil	____ destroyed

Road Signs

Circle the 8 signs you might see as you drive down the highway.

Ferry to Isle Royale	Crown Point City Limits	Tony Boyle
Hotpoint Service Center	Oyster Bay Welcomes You	Boycott Water
William DuBois	Re-elect Senator Moynihan	The Real McCoy
Leaving Doylestown Come Back Soon	Ohio Turnpike Next Left	Visit Historic Croyden

An oi/oy Story

Leroy and Joy Poindexter live on Burgoyne Street in Troy, Iowa. They have a son named Floyd and a little girl named Joyce. The children's birthdays fall on the same day, and that can present problems sometimes.

Joyce wants monsters for her birthday, The Noid and Tacky Stretchoid. Floyd says he wants tapes of rock stars, any or all of the following: "Hanoi Rocks," "Art of Noise," "Noiseworks," "Nightnoise," "Oingo Boingo," "Midnight Oil," or "The Right Choice." He also wants a Polaroid camera.

As an extra treat, they want to eat out and see a movie. Joyce would choose "Monstroids;" "Gerald McBoing-Boing" would be a second choice. Floyd wants to see nothing but "Murder Ahoy" or "Destroyer." Mrs. Poindexter would like to see "Royal Love Story," but it isn't her birthday.

Floyd wants to eat at The Boiler Room, but Joyce says she won't go if she can't eat at the Rolls-Royce Burger. Mr. Poindexter prefers the Blue Oyster, but it isn't his birthday, either.

It gets to be all too much for the Poindexter parents. Joy says they will eat at home. She will get a fancy cake at the In Joy bakery. Floyd can go to the Joyride Record Shop and pick three tapes. Leroy will take Joyce to Toys-R-Us® for two monsters. They all play a game of quoits in the backyard and later get out the game of "Clip Joint." The children telephone their grandparents in Beloit and Boyne. When the day is over, Joyce says she has enjoyed the day, and Floyd agrees.

Chapter 5
au and *aw*

au as in **Paul** (pôl)	*aw* as in **saw** (sô)

Sound and Spelling

1. The Sound of *au* as in **Paul** and *aw* as in **saw**

au and *aw* have the same sound.

Write the words that have the same vowel sound and the same consonant ending as the numbered word.

brawl	crawl	dawn	drawn	fawn	flaw
haul	pawn	slaw	straw	thaw	vault

1. lawn _____ _____ _____ _____

2. saw _____ _____ _____ _____

3. Paul _____ _____ _____

4. fault _____

Read sentences with some of these words and others with *au* and *aw*.

1. <u>Paul</u> opened the heavy bank <u>vault</u> door.

2. Why did he <u>scrawl</u> his name on my <u>pawn</u> ticket?

3. The mother deer watched her little <u>fawn</u> as the <u>hawk</u> swooped down.

4. <u>Saul's</u> pit bull would <u>maul</u> another dog savagely.

5. Maud found a flaw in the shirt and returned it.

6. He was drawn into a big brawl at the bar, but he wasn't badly hurt.

7. We put up a squawk about what a fraud the sale was.

8. Dawn tripped over a wire that was pulled taut.

Longer, Common Words with *au*

Write in *au* and read the words.

1. l __ __ ndry	**5.** l __ __ nder	**9.** exh __ __ st	**13.** __ __ thor
2. f __ __ lty	**6.** d __ __ ghter	**10.** __ __ to	**14.** appl __ __ se
3. s __ __ sage	**7.** s __ __ cer	**11.** f __ __ cet	**15.** apples __ __ ce
4. s __ __ na	**8.** __ __ gust	**12.** bec __ __ se	**16.** __ __ tumn

Longer, Common Words with *aw*

Write in *aw* and read the words.

1. dr __ __ er	**3.** __ __ kward	**5.** __ __ ning	**7.** jigs __ __
2. l __ __ yer	**4.** __ __ ful	**6.** fl __ __ less	**8.** withdr __ __ n

2. Spelling *au* and *aw* Words

As with the other vowels you have been handling so far in this book, you can't tell which pair to write just by listening for the sound. *au* and *aw* sound alike, and you may have to look in more than one place to find a word in the dictionary or telephone book.

Write the words and add *ing*, *ed*, and *er*.

> Do not double the last letter.

1. haul   _____, _____, _____

2. brawl   _____, _____, _____

3. launder   _____, _____, _____

4. exhaust   _____, _____ (Do not add *er*.)

Syllables and Accents

1.   Writing Words in Syllables

Write the words in syllables and put in the main accents.

1. restaurant   _____ _____ _____
2. overhaul   _____ _____ _____
3. manslaughter   _____ _____ _____
4. somersault   _____ _____ _____
5. Laundromat   _____ _____ _____
6. autopsy   _____ _____ _____
7. auditor   _____ _____ _____
8. awkwardly   _____ _____ _____
9. unlawful   _____ _____ _____
10. awfully   _____ _____ _____
11. strawberry   _____ _____ _____
12. naughtiness   _____ _____ _____

2. Word Building

Mark the syllables with slashes and put in the main accent. Read the sentences.

1. **auto automate automatic automotive**

   A car is rarely called an <u>auto</u>. Workers will be laid off when the company <u>automates</u> the assembly line. Our elevator has no attendant; it is <u>automatic</u>. He works in an <u>automotive</u> plant.

2. **author authorship authorize authority authoritative**

   Who is the <u>author</u> of this book? The <u>authorship</u> of the book is unknown. Did the parents <u>authorize</u> letting him go on the trip? On whose <u>authority</u> are you taking the car? The new chairman spoke in a very <u>authoritative</u> manner to the foreman.

3. **audit auditor audible auditory**

   The bank examiners came to <u>audit</u> the books. One <u>auditor</u> found a mistake that was very strange. Your voice is barely <u>audible</u> over the telephone. She suffered <u>auditory</u> nerve damage and can't hear well.

4. **exhaust exhausted exhaustive exhaustible**

   Working twelve hours a day would <u>exhaust</u> anybody. I <u>exhausted</u> all my funds. The sheriff made an <u>exhaustive</u> search for the gun. Fresh water, oil, and coal are all <u>exhaustible</u>, so we had best save them.

3. Split-Vowel Words

When you reverse **au**, you no longer have paired vowels: **dual** (du′ al), **truant** (tru′ ant), **evacuate** (e vac′ u ate), or **continual** (con tin′ u al). These words were studied in *Handling Words, Book 1*.

iu, eu, io, ia

Write the words in syllables.

1. audio   _____ _____ _____

2. Claudia   _____ _____ _____

3. Austria   _____ _____ _____

4. mausoleum   _____ _____ _____ _____

5. auditorium   _____ _____ _____ _____ _____

6. authoritarian   _____ _____ _____ _____ _____

    _____

Read these words in sentences.

1. My sister <u>Claudia</u> heard a good program in the <u>auditorium</u>.

2. The <u>audio</u> part of our TV set isn't working.

3. A rich family built a <u>mausoleum</u> in the cemetery for their dead.

4. <u>Austria</u>, a small country south of Germany, was under Hitler's cruel <u>authoritarian</u> government during World War II.

Dictionary Marks and Less-Common Words

> **Paul** (pôl) and **saw** (sô)

The dictionary respells **au** and **aw** with **ô**, like the **o** in **log** (lôg), like the **ar** in **war** (wôr), and like the **or** in **corn** (kôrn).

1. Learning the Markings with Words You Know

Write the words after the respellings. Try to spell the words without looking at the following list.

draw   fault   haul   law   pawn   slaw

1. pôn _____

2. fôlt _____

3. slô _____

4. drô _____

5. hôl _____

6. lô _____

2. Writing Less-Common Words

Write the words after the respellings.

auburn   authentic   awesome   brawny   caustic   default

gaudy   Holocaust   inaugurate   jaundice   plausible   thesaurus

1. gô′ dē _____

2. ô then′ tik _____

3. di fôlt′ _____

4. ô′ bərn _____

5. jôn′ dis _____

6. hol′ ə kôst′ _____

7. kôs′ tik _____

8. plô′ zə b'l _____

9. brôn′ ē _____

10. in ô′ gyə rāt′ _____

11. ô′ səm _____

12. thi sôr′ əs _____

Read these words in sentences.

1. The picture is not <u>authentic</u>; it is just a copy.

2. Masses of Jews and others died in the <u>Holocaust</u>.

58

3. Your liver is not healthy if you have <u>jaundice</u>.

4. A tornado touching down is an <u>awesome</u> thing to see.

5. They didn't make the house payments, so it was lost by <u>default</u>.

6. You can learn many new words from a <u>thesaurus</u>, a kind of dictionary.

7. We <u>inaugurate</u> a president every four years, but not always a new one.

8. The woman with <u>auburn</u> hair was burned by <u>caustic</u> cleaning liquid.

9. She told a <u>plausible</u> story, but some people didn't believe it.

10. The big <u>brawny</u> man was dressed in a <u>gaudy</u> red and pink shirt.

3. Out-of-Pattern and Other Confusing Words

☆ Two **au** words have the short **a** sound, as most people say it: **laugh** (laf) and **aunt** (ant).

☆ In **gauge** (gāj), you hear long **a**.

☆ In a few words that come from French, **au** makes the long **o** sound:

- **chauffeur** (shō′ fər) and **chauvinists** (shō′ və nists), people who have extreme views about their own country, race, or sex.

Little Words in Longer Words

Write on a piece of paper the little words in the following names of places.

1. Hawkins	4. Hawthorne	7. Rawsonville	10. Lauderhill
2. Crawley	5. Saginaw	8. Warsaw	11. Lawton
3. Clawson	6. Washtenaw	9. Chicasaw	12. Saugatuck

"How Do You Say Your Name?"

Names from the British Isles with **au** have the sound you have learned in this chapter: Laurel, Lauren, Pauley. However, names coming from Germany have the sound of **ou** as in **out**: Auer, Muldaur, Nicklaus, Metzenbaum. People with such names are accustomed to telling you how to say their names, and many people use the English way of saying **au**. In names from France, **au** has the long **o** sound, Aumont, but Americans rarely bother with pronouncing such names the French way.

Read the names and listen to the sound of *au* and *aw*:

Lawler	Clauson	Lawrence
Autry	Faulkner	Caudill
Dawes	Staunton	Audubon

Handling *au* and *aw* Words . . . Lightly

Place Names

Many places on the map have the first name of a person. <u>Mark out the 20 place names that</u> <u>are</u> ***not*** <u>first names.</u>

Milwaukee	Lawrence	Escatawpa	Waukegan
Maumee	Maureen	Paula	Kennesaw
Claudia	Sawhill	Mohawk	Paw Paw
Wausau	Maud	Choctaw	Audrey
Pawnee	Dinosaur	Austria	Laureen
Wauwatosa	Claude	Chauncey	Gnaw Bone
Paul	Shawnee	Slaughter	Laura
Massauga	Dawn	Chautauqua	Secaucus

Headlines

<u>Check 7 headlines that would confuse George Washington if he returned.</u>

____ 1. Flying <u>Saucer</u> Spotted over Fort <u>Lauderdale</u>

____ 2. Man Charged with <u>Assault</u>

____ 3. <u>U-Haul</u> and <u>Haul-Away</u> Crash on Interstate 90

____ 4. <u>Audio</u> Store Opens near <u>Auto</u> Plant

____ 5. Boston <u>Inaugurates</u> New Mayor

____ 6. *Dirty Laundry*, Showing Locally, Rated R

____ 7. President Gives Long <u>Inaugural</u> Speech

____ 8. <u>Automatic</u> Teller Robbed in <u>Austin</u>, Texas

____ 9. President's <u>Authority</u> Put to Test

____ 10. Truck Runs into Squeeky-Kleen <u>Laundromat</u>

____ 11. <u>Astronauts</u> Land Space Shuttle Safely

____ 12. <u>Shawnee</u> and <u>Ottawa</u> Indians Demand Rights

Judgment Words

Using some words can cause an argument because they show judgment on the part of the user. Other words simply describe or state what is certain. Circle the word (or words) that might make someone disagree with you.

naughty boy	dawdling worker	autumn leaves
kitchen faucet	withdrawn child	striped awning
plausible reason	gauze bandage	August days
authoritarian father	awesome thunderstorm	scrawny woman
sausage	assault and battery	awful job
restaurant	automatic teller	applause
awkward dancer	fraudulent deal	cauliflower
somersaults	auditory nerves	faulty product

Classic Movies

Circle the titles of 8 movies, some of them made a long time ago, but which appear on television from time to time.

The Pawnbroker	Audubon Bird Drawings
The Prince and the Pauper	Little Lord Fauntleroy
Slaughterhouse 5	Keys to Surviving a Tax Audit
The Awful Truth	The Causes of Jaundice
Lawrence of Arabia	Drums Along the Mohawk
Laura Ashley's Home Design	The Outlaw

Science Words

Mark out the 8 words you would *not* likely read in a science-class textbook.

astronauts	bauxite	auditory nerves	somersaults
dinosaurs	lawyers	trauma	heehaw
exhaust	Santa Claus	applesauce	earthquake faults
jaundice	laundry	sausage	Austin, TX

62

Chapter 6
Two More Sounds
of *a*

a as in **talk** (tôk)	*a* as in **father** (fä′ thər)

Sound and Spelling

1. The Sound of *a* as in **talk**

This is the sound you hear in **for**, **war**, **dog**, and **saw**.
Words with *al*, *all*, *alk* often have the *a* as in **talk** sound.

Write the words that have the same vowel sound and the same consonant ending as the numbered word.

> Some words have a silent *l*.

balk   ball   chalk   fall   mall   malt
salt   scald   stalk   stall   walk   Walt

1. talk   _____   _____   _____   _____

2. all   _____   _____   _____   _____

3. halt   _____   _____   _____

4. bald   _____

Read sentences with some of these words and others with the *a* as in talk sound.

1. A cat will <u>stalk</u> a bird. A whole <u>stalk</u> of celery goes into the stew.

2. Before winter, we <u>calk</u> the windows to make them tight.

3. I <u>balk</u> at riding in a car that might <u>stall</u> in traffic.

4. You hear a baby <u>squall</u>. Wind with rain is called a <u>squall</u>.

5. The cloth put over a coffin is a <u>pall</u>.

6. <u>Walt</u> made a chocolate <u>malt</u> with skim milk.

Longer, Common Words with *a* as in talk

Write in *a* and read the words.

1. w __ lnut

2. __ lso

3. __ lmost

4. f __ lse

5. w __ ltz

6. __ lways

7. sm __ llpox

8. inst __ ll

9. __ llspice

10. h __ lter

11. h __ llway

12. f __ lsely

13. f __ llen

14. __ lter (change)

15. __ ltar (in a church)

64

2. The Sound of *a* as in **father**

This is the sound heard in **lot** (lot) and **car** (kär).

Circle the 8 words that have the sound of *a* as in father. Some of the words have the long *a* as in cake and the short *a* as in bad. Do not circle them.

palm	stamp	shake	squad	what	that	strange	squash	scrap
paste	squat	valve	quake	swatch	match	calm	sank	swat

> The sound of *a* often varies from one part of the country to another. A few words in which you would hear either *a* as in **father** or *a* as in **talk** are: **watch, wash, squad, swat, calm, swamp, wander, swan, wad, squander, watt, waffle, wallet**, and **want.** Dictionaries may show two ways of saying these words, both acceptable.

Read sentences with some of these words and others with the *a* as in father or the *a* as in talk sound.

1. Be on the watch if you swat at a bee and miss.

2. He ran the palm of his hand over the smooth trunk of the palm tree.

3. Wash the squash before cooking it.

4. The football squad's room had only a 40-watt bulb for light.

5. With great calm, the captain told his men to squat down very low.

6. Make a wad of this little swatch of fabric to see if it wrinkles.

7. He would wander into town and squander all his money in a night.

8. A lovely white swan appeared on the black swamp water.

Longer, Common Words with *a* as in **father**

Write in *a* and read the words.

1. m __ ma
3. sw __ llow
5. mass __ ge
7. qu __ ntity

2. p __ pa
4. cors __ ge
6. gar __ ge
8. qu __ lity

3.   Spelling *a* as in **father** and *a* as in **talk** Words

> Since there are other letters (*or, o,*
> and *ar*) that spell these *a* sounds,
> you may have to look in several
> places in the dictionary and
> telephone book. The silent *l* in some
> of these words must be remembered.

Write the words and add *ing*, *ed*, and *er*.

> Follow the rule for short vowels in
> doubling the last consonant if only
> one follows the vowel.

1. walk   _____ _____ _____

2. squat _____ _____ _____

3. calm   _____ _____ _____

4. wad   _____ _____ (Do not add *er*)

5. watch _____ _____ _____

66

Syllables and Accents

1. Writing Words in Syllables

Write the words in syllables and put in the main accent marks.

1. wallpaper   _____ _____ _____

2. saltshaker   _____ _____ _____

3. talkative   _____ _____ _____

4. watchfulness   _____ _____ _____

5. fatherhood   _____ _____ _____

6. saltiness   _____ _____ _____

7. installment   _____ _____ _____

8. gallbladder   _____ _____ _____

9. washable   _____ _____ _____

10. quality   _____ _____ _____

11. quantity   _____ _____ _____

12. pallbearer   _____ _____ _____

Dictionary Marks and Less-Common Words

> *a* as in **talk** (tôk) and
> *a* as in **father** fä′ thər)

The sound of *a* as in **talk** (tôk) is respelled the same way as *o* in **log** (lôg).
It is the sound heard in **saw** (sô).
The sound of *a* as in **father** (fä′thər) is the same respelling you saw in
car (kär). Some dictionaries respell the short *o* with *ä*: lot (lät).

1. Learning the Markings with Words You Know

Write the word after the respelling. Try to spell the words without looking at the following list.

all	bald	calm	mall	salt	scald
squash	squat	swatch	wad	watt	what

1. bôld _____

2. skôld _____

3. hwät _____

4. wät _____

5. wäd _____

6. ôl _____

7. swäch _____

8. käm _____

9. sôlt _____

10. môl _____

11. skwät _____

12. skwäsh _____

2. Writing Less-Common Words

Write the word in the blank before the respelling.

alderman	almanac	appalled	Balkans
balsa	Baltic	cobalt	falter

1. Sweden and Finland are on the _____ (bôl′ tik) Sea.

2. Model airplanes are made of the very light _____ (bôl′ sə) wood.

3. The dancer had hurt her leg, but she still did not _____ (fôl′ tər).

4. We were _____ (ə pôld′) by the number of smashed cars.

5. Iron and nickel are found in _____ (kō′ bôlt).

6. The _____ (bôl′ kənz) are lands just south and east of Austria.

7. In some cities, a city councilperson is called an

_____ (ôl′ dər mən).

8. I look up many facts in my latest _____ (ôl′ mə nak′)

Write the words after the respellings.

embalm	Islam	lager	lava	Slavic
squabble	squadron	squalor	swastika	Talmud

1. läv′ ə _____

2. lä′ gər _____

3. im bäm′ _____

4. skwäl′ ər _____

5. is läm′ _____

6. skwäd′ rən _____

7. täl′ mood _____

8. swäs′ ti kə _____

9. släv′ ik _____

10. skwäb′ ′l _____

Read these words in sentences.

1. A volcano throws up melted rock called <u>lava</u>.

2. The brewery makes German <u>lager</u>.

3. You must have a license before you can <u>embalm</u> a body.

4. The ragged man was very rich, but he lived in utter <u>squalor</u>.

5. The holy book of <u>Islam</u> is the *Koran*.

6. We heard a <u>squadron</u> of bombers fly over last night.

7. The Jewish book of laws is called the *<u>Talmud</u>*.

8. A <u>swastika</u>, a cross with bent arms, is no longer a good luck sign.

9. Polish people are <u>Slavic</u>, as are most people in the former U.S.S.R.

10. The children got into a great <u>squabble</u> over who would get the most candy.

"How Do You Say Your Name?"

Saying people's names with a single *a* leaves you some choices, but you rarely make a mistake. Whether you say *a* as in **father** or *a* as in **talk**, the listener can understand you.

Say the names of famous people both ways and listen to the close sounds.

Caldwell	Calder	Calkins	Sinatra	Walters	Swanson
Salk	Bacall	Baldwin	Palmer	Dukakis	Balsam
Waddles	Alston	Waldron	Walls	Watson	Watkins

Handling More a Words . . . Lightly

Books into Movies

Circle the titles of books that were or could be made into movies.

The Godfather

The Great Waltz

Politics of Nepal

Rose of Panama

Two Wanderers

The Saint of Palm
Springs

Plants and Animals
of Walden Pond

The Alderman

Night Stalker

Quality Street

The Tightwad

Life With Father

History of Topkapi
Palace

The Baltic
Republics and the
U.S.S.R.

The Squall

The Swan

A Fish Called
Wanda

Moonlight on the
Wabash

Wasps, Bees, and
Flowers

The Quantum
Theory of
Energy

Death at Lake
Tahoe

Getting a Job

Read the story.

Tanya Walters comes from Walled Lake to Baltimore looking for work. She asks at the Ramada Inn, Dalton Books, and Walgreen's Drugstore. She isn't trained to work at the Wigwam Hair Shop. She doesn't want to work at the Wander Inn or Ba-Ba-Ree-Ba Club or Grandma's Saloon. She has seen too many people getting swashed, embalmed, gaga, or whatever getting drunk is called.

Tanya considers a record store. In the window are albums of The Talking Heads, The Fire Squad, Muddy Waters, and Taj Mahal. Blaring away inside the shop are The Wee Papa Girls and Mama's Boys, both playing at the same time. This is not for her.

Tanya goes to the nearest place to eat. She has almond waffles and avocado salad. The manager needs help and hires her. Tanya is happy and will write home. Will her dad in Walled Lake understand she is working at My Father's Place, in Baltimore?

Street Names

When a new part of a city opens up, street names must be chosen. <u>Underline names you would choose for new streets.</u>

Albany	Wanda	Almost	Granada	Palmolive
Swap	Wad	Wallop	Pall Mall	Quality
Walnut	Kumquat	Tanya	Tahoe	Caldwell
Bra	Swamp	Balmy	Yolanda	Kirkendall
Waldorf	Quadruplet	Kilowatt	Amen	Palm Grove

Looking for a Job

<u>Circle the 11 places you might look for a job.</u> Some of the names are groups that are staffed mainly by volunteers; don't circle them.

Dalton Books	Aqua World	Auto Plaza
Quality Pest Control	Fathers for Equal Rights	Suwanee Leather Co.
Chimney Rescue Squad	Cerebral Palsy Support Group	Walgreen's Drug Store
Kiwanis Club	Ramada Inn	Walker's Club
An Ultimate Message	Food Squad	Mother Waddles' Haven for the Homeless
Slavic Students Club	Yamaha Motorsports	

Having a Holiday

<u>Circle 7 places you could have a camping holiday.</u>

Lava Hot Springs, CA	Lake Tahoe, NV	Washington, D.C.
Walnut Canyon, AZ	Albany's Empire Plaza, NY	Walden Pond, MA
Okefenokee Swamp, GA	Amana colonies in Iowa	Baltimore, MD
Minnehaha Falls, MN	Baldwin Lake, MI	Omaha, NB

Chapter 7
OU and *OW*

ou as in **out** (out)   ow as in **how** (hou)

ou as in **group** (grōop) ou as in **soul** (sōl)
ou as in **bought** (bôt)   ou as in **enough** (i nuf´)
ou as in **could** (kood)

Sound and Spelling

1. The Sound of *ou* as in **out** and *ow* as in **how**

The most common sound of *ou* is heard in **out**. *ou* and *ow* have the same sound in many words.

Write the words that have the same vowel sound and the same consonant ending as the numbered word.

blouse	bound	clown	couch	crouch	drown	fowl	frown	grouch
hound	mouse	owl	pound	prowl	scour	sour	town	

1. sound   _____, _____, _____

2. house   _____, _____

3. ouch   _____, _____, _____

4. our   _____, _____

5. down   _____, _____, _____, _____

6. howl   _____, _____, _____

Read sentences with some of these words and others that have the _ou_ as in out and _ow_ as in how sound.

1. <u>Our</u> teacher was a <u>grouch</u>, always saying, "Don't <u>slouch</u> in your seat!"

2. The cat <u>pounced</u> on the <u>mouse</u> and dashed under the <u>couch</u>.

3. He had to <u>shout</u> in a <u>loud</u> voice, "<u>Douse</u> the fire, now!"

4. There was only <u>sour</u> milk and not even an <u>ounce</u> of meat in the <u>house</u>.

5. Why does he <u>prowl</u> around here with a mean <u>scowl</u> on his face?

6. I <u>vow</u> I'll never kill a <u>fowl</u> again, chicken or turkey.

7. A little <u>owl</u> was stitched on the front of her long <u>gown</u>.

Longer, Common Words with _ou_ as in out

Write in _ou_ and read the words.

1. ar __ __ nd	4. tr __ __ sers	7. m __ __ ntain	10. c __ __ nty
2. al __ __ d	5. surr __ __ nd	8. ann __ __ nce	11. pron __ __ nce
3. am __ __ nt	6. f __ __ ntain	9. disc __ __ nt	12. th __ __ sand

Longer, Common Words with _ow_ as in how

Write in _ow_ and read the words.

1. fl __ __ er	3. t __ __ el	5. c __ __ ard	7. ch __ __ der
2. p __ __ er	4. v __ __ el	6. all __ __	8. t __ __ nship

2. Other Sounds of _ou_ as in **group**, as in **bought**, as in **soul**, as in **enough** and as in **could**

> There aren't many words in each of these _ou_ groups, but most of them are important words to read and spell.

74

Write the words that have the same vowel sound and the same consonant ending as the numbered word.

> *gh* is silent in some words; in others, *gh* has the sound of *f*. Watch for silent *l* in some words.

brought	fought	ought	rough	soup
should	though	thought	tough	would

1. bought _____ _____ _____ _____
2. group _____
3. could _____ _____
4. enough _____ _____
5. dough _____

Read sentences with some of these words and others that have the sounds of *ou*.

1. Though he is a tough fellow with rough ways, I like him.

2. The baby could not breathe well; we thought she had croup.

3. She brought cold water in a hollowed-out gourd for us to drink from.

4. The young man took a tour with a group to the source of the Mississippi.

5. You should not touch the bread dough while it is rising.

6. The state sought to help the poor with volunteers, but it came to nought.

Longer, Common Words with the Other *ou* Sounds

Write in *ou* and read the word.

> You must try out the many sounds of *ou*: as in **group**, **bought**, **soul**, **enough** or **could**. In three words, *gh* is silent.

1. s __ __ thern
2. t __ __ rist
3. c __ __ sin
4. y __ __ ngster
5. c __ __ ntry

6. tr __ __ ble
7. c __ __ ple
8. c __ __ pon
9. b __ __ levard
10. thor __ __ gh

11. sh __ __ lder
12. alth __ __ gh
13. d __ __ ble
14. s __ __ venir
15. b __ __ lder

16. det __ __ r
17. L __ __ is
18. furl __ __ gh
19. D __ __ glas
20. cantal __ __ pe

3. Spelling *ou* and *ow* Words

> When looking up a word, you must look for *ou*, *ow*, and the other ways of spelling the sounds represented by these two tricky pairs. The "Dictionary Marks" part of this chapter will help you with this.

Write the words and add *ing* and *ed*.

1. sour   _____, _____
2. howl   _____, _____
3. group   _____, _____
4. detour   _____, _____

Write the words and add *s* or *es*.

1. county _____
2. country _____
3. pound _____
4. house _____
5. couch _____
6. pronounce _____

Syllables and Accents

1. Writing Words in Syllables

Write the words in syllables and put in the main accent marks.

1. youthful _____ _____
2. powerful _____ _____ _____
3. announcement _____ _____ _____
4. mispronounce _____ _____ _____
5. troublesome _____ _____ _____
6. doubtless _____ _____
7. nourishment _____ _____ _____
8. sourness _____ _____
9. cowardly _____ _____ _____
10. encouragement _____ _____ _____ _____
11. thoughtfulness _____ _____ _____
12. tournament _____ _____ _____

2. An *ou* Prefix/Beginning

counter (meaning against or opposite) as in **counteract**

This prefix/beginning has two syllables.

Write the words in syllables.

1. counteract   _____ _____ _____

2. countersign   _____ _____ _____

3. counterbalance   _____ _____ _____ _____

4. counterclockwise   _____ _____ _____ _____

Read these words in sentences.

1. She took medicine to <u>counteract</u> the sneezing from hay fever.

2. I had to <u>countersign</u> the bank loan for my son.

3. Engineers must <u>counterbalance</u> the drawbridge or it won't swing up to let boats through.

4. Moving opposite the way clock hands go is moving <u>counterclockwise</u>.

3.   An *ou* Suffix/Ending: ***ous*** as in **famous**

> The sound of ***ous*** is ***us***. It is a separate syllable and not accented.

Match the related words and put in the main accent mark.

cancerous	courageous	famous	dangerous	hazardous
humorous	mountainous	nervous	numerous	poisonous

1. fame _____

2. nerve _____

3. hazard _____

4. poison _____

5. courage _____

6. danger _____

7. cancer _____

8. number _____

9. mountain _____

10. humor _____

4. Split Vowels in *ous* Words

Write the words in syllables.

1. serious   _____ _____ _____

2. strenuous _____ _____ _____

3. tedious   _____ _____ _____

4. courteous _____ _____ _____

5. conspicuous _____ _____ _____

                                    _____

6. continuous _____ _____ _____

                                    _____

7. delirious   _____ _____ _____

                                    _____

8. miscellaneous _____ _____ _____

                                    _____ _____

Read some of these words in sentences.

1. Even walking was too <u>strenuous</u> for the old man.

2. We call things that don't fit in any other group <u>miscellaneous</u> things.

3. He was <u>delirious</u> from high fever and talked utter nonsense.

4. Waiting in a traffic jam is as <u>tedious</u> as listening to some speeches.

5. They make themselves <u>conspicuous</u> by loud talking and laughing.

6. Even with the <u>continuous</u> flow of people, the clerk was <u>courteous</u>.

5. *ous* Words and the Shifted Accent

Change *y* to *i* and add *ous*. Put in the accent marks in all words.

> ☞ **Remember:** Accents often shift when an ending is added.

1. envy _____

2. glory _____

3. victory _____

4. vary _____

5. injury _____

6. industry _____

Dictionary Marks and Less-Common Words

> **out** (out)
> **how** (hou)
> **group** (gro͞op)
> **brought** (brôt)
> **enough** (i nuf′)
> **soul** (sōl)
> **could** (ko͝od)

> If you are having trouble finding **ou** or **ow** words in the dictionary or telephone book, you may have to look for words with the long or short **u** and **o**. You might have to look in the **oo** words, and, of course, you must look for both **ou** and **ow** spellings.

1. Learning the Markings with Words You Know

Write the word after the respelling. Try to write the words without looking at the list.

dough	drown	house	howl	mouse	rough
soup	sour	though	thought	tough	would

1. hous _____
2. droun _____
3. thôt _____
4. wood _____
5. houl _____
6. so͞op _____

7. thō _____
8. ruf _____
9. do͞o _____
10. mous _____
11. sour _____
12. tuf _____

2. Writing Less-Common Words

ou and *ow*

Write the word after the respelling.

allowance	astound	bounty	Bowery	endowment
devour	devout	gouge	impound	pronoun

1. gouj   _____

2. ə lou′ əns _____

3. di vour′ _____

4. boun′ tē _____

5. bou′ ər ē _____

6. prō′ noun   _____

7. im pound′   _____

8. di vout′   _____

9. ə stound′   _____

10. in dou′ mənt _____

Read these words in sentences.

1. The boy used his new knife to <u>gouge</u> little holes in the chair.

2. The <u>Bowery</u> is a street in New York with many bars and poor drunks.

3. A cloud of locusts will <u>devour</u> every grain of wheat in the fields.

4. To protect the chickens, a <u>bounty</u> was given to fox-killing hunters.

5. The <u>pronoun</u> *she* is used in place of a female's name.

6. If they <u>impound</u> your car, you must pay for the towing and storage.

7. She goes to church every day; she is very <u>devout</u>.

8. The teenagers <u>astound</u> me by how much they can eat.

9. Her husband gave her an <u>allowance</u> but no charge card.

10. The college used the wealthy man's <u>endowment</u> of money to pay for the lab.

The Other *ou* Sounds

Write the words in the blanks.

bourbon   coupling   croutons   nougat
poultry   velour   vermouth   wrought

1. They made _____ (noo′ gət) candy with honey and almonds.

2. You may find duck and turkey in the _____ (pōl′ trē) department.

3. The trainman tightened a loose _____ (kup′ liŋ) between the cars.

4. The county in Kentucky where _____ (bʉr′ bən) whiskey is made was named for French kings.

5. Wine flavored with herbs is called _____ (vər mooth′)

6. Make _____ (kroo′ tons) for soup by cutting bread into little cubes.

7. A _____ (və loor′) shirt feels and looks very much like velvet.

8. The _____ (rôt) iron fence was painted white.

More Words with the Other *ou* Sounds

Write the words after the respellings.

acoustical   borough   contour   goulash   louver   mourns   poultice   trough

1. bʉr′ ō _____
2. trôf _____
3. môrns _____
4. loo′ vər _____

5. kon′ toor _____
6. goo′ läsh _____
7. ə koos′ tik ′l _____
8. pōl′ tis _____

Read the words in sentences.

1. Two slats in the <u>louver</u> window are broken.

2. They put <u>acoustical</u> tile in the office to keep down the noise.

3. The Bronx is the most northern <u>borough</u> of New York City.

4. A <u>contour</u> chair fits the shape of the body.

5. We ate a stew called Hungarian <u>goulash</u>.

6. A <u>poultice</u> of tea leaves on your black eye may help.

7. The table looks as neat as a pig <u>trough</u>.

8. On Memorial Day, our country <u>mourns</u> the dead of all wars.

3. Out-of-Pattern and Other Confusing Words

☆ Dictionaries differ in the way they show the sounds of a few *ou* words (**tournament, four, course, route**, for example), but the sounds are very close and don't cause much trouble.

☆ In a few important words, an *r* following *ou* changes the sound:

- I took a long **journey** (jur′ nē) by train.

- I write in a **journal** (jur′ n'l) every day.

- It took great **courage** (kur′ ij) to go into battle.

- The people of the lodge always treated me with **courtesy** (kur′ tə sē).

- We **nourish** (nur′ ish) our children with food and with love.

There are a few more.

☆ *ow* in a very few, but common, words has two sounds, depending on the sense of the sentence.

- You tie a **bow**. (long *o*) You take a **bow** for a job well done.

- You **row** a boat. You have a big **row** with the boss and get fired.

☆ In the following words, the sound of *ow* changes when one or more letters are added or changed.

- I will **show** you something after you take your **shower**.

- I watched the river **flow** by as I picked a **flower**.

- My anger **grows** when that dog **growls** at us.

- Get the truck to **tow** the car away from the water **tower**.

- The fire's warm **glow** turned his mean **glower** into a smile.

☆ In a few words, the sound of *ou* changes when one or more letters are added or changed.

- **south** (south) and **southern** (suth′ərn)

- **court** (kôrt) and **courtesy** (kur′ tə se)

- **brought** (brôt) and **drought** (drout)

- **soul** (sōl) and **foul** (foul)

- **cough** (kôf) and **rough** (ruf)

- **sour** (sour) and **source** (sôrs)

There are not many more.

☆ The word **wound** has two meanings and sounds:

- Yesterday you **wound** (wound) your watch.

- The **wound** (wo͞ond) won't heal.

☆ And, once again, those four confusing **ou** words, **though** (thō), **thought** (thôt), **through** (thro͞o), and **thorough** (thŭr′ō)

- though   I like swimming, <u>though</u> I don't do much now.

- thought   I <u>thought</u> of you.

- through   I am <u>through</u> working. I went <u>through</u> the door.

- thorough   The doctor gave me a <u>thorough</u> exam.

''How Do You Say Your Name?''

People whose names have **ou** or **ow** in them are frequently asked how to pronounce their names. If the name is well known or there is a common word in the name, you can make a good try. But since many names have more than one way of saying them, nobody needs to feel uneasy about asking. Below are some names of famous people, as well as names you may never have heard before.

Circle the names you have doubts about pronouncing.

Powers	Dow	Burroughs	Downey	Kow
Houston	Browning	Houchens	Gould	Crowley
Brougher	McDowell	O'Rourke	Finkhouser	Goudee
Harcourt	Bowers	Calhoun	Townsend	Houghton

Handling *ou* and *ow* Words . . . Lightly

Places to Visit

Place names with **ou** and **ow** often leave you in doubt as to how to say them. A large dictionary will help you pronounce some of the names, but asking the local people is the only way in some cases. Circle the places you might want to visit some day.

Moscow, ID	The Rocky Mountains	Grand Coulee Dam, WA
Opelousas, LA in the winter	The airport concourse at Louisville, KY	A St. Louis, Missouri zoo
The Lost and Found Saloon in Bourbon, IN	The Astrodome in Houston, TX	The Cow Palace in San Francisco, CA
The fishing bridge at Pascagoula, MS	The Moucho Poocho Shop in Boulevard, CA	An iron foundry in Youngstown, OH
A tourist trap in Missoula, MT	The Battleground at Vicksburg, MS	The White House, DC and Mount Vernon, VA
An Indian powwow in Council Bluffs, IA	The Apartment Lounge in Baton Rouge, LA	The bay and city park in Vancouver, Canada

Book Titles

Circle the 12 titles of books that are stories.

The Hill of Evil Counsel	Uncommon Vows	Parent Resource Guide
The Fountainhead	The Benefit of the Doubt	New Orleans Mourning
Journey to the Center of the Earth	Boundaries	The Perfect Furlough
Dirty Rotten Scoundrels	The Nine Most Troublesome Teenage Problems	Golf Tours and Detours
Rough and Tender		Shroud for a Nightingale
A Sewing Course	How to Save Your Troubled Marriage	Famous Tennis Tournaments
	Mutiny on the Bounty	

What's a Good Employee?

Check the 10 words that an employer might look for in hiring.

serious	courageous	grouchy	jealous
industrious	ridiculous	sour	thoughtful
mournful	furious	sound	well-nourished
curious	cantankerous	resourceful	bourbon-drinking
courteous	rowdy	nervous	conspicuous
thorough	troublesome	envious	adulterous

Telephone Book Listings

The following are listed in the "business" part of the telephone book. Some are businesses, operating for profit. Others are nonprofit groups to help people. Some of them are government agencies of one sort or another. Circle the 8 profit-making listings.

District and Circuit Courts

The Cat's Meow

Doubleday Book Shop

Toughlove, an Approach to Parenting

Thoroughbred Lounge

Hazardous Substance Panel

Sourdough Baker

Astounding Clowning

Resolve Through Sharing

Boy Scouts' Council

AIDS Testing and Counseling Service

Downtown Task Force

Mothers' Community Resource Center

V.A. Accounts Payable

Fabulous Food

Soundings: Center for Women

Discount Batteries

Pigs' Trough Lounge

Have You Ever Wondered . . .

If dogs like to eat horehound-flavored cough drops?

If a journeyman carpenter ever goes on a journey?

If the skin on a roughneck's neck is smooth?

If a court plaster is made of plaster and worn only in court?

If a cowboy ever grows up to become a cowman?

If a housewarming gets too hot in the summer?

How much teasing people get who live in Yellow House, Pie Town, Cowpens, Trout, Cattown, and Coward?

How we got the sayings "froufrou" and "kowtow"?

If people say "hoosgow" instead of jail because it sounds less serious?

Chapter 8
ie and *ei*

> *ie* as in **yield** (yēld)   *ei* as in **neither** (nē′ thər)
>
> *ei* as in **eight** (āt)   *ie* as in **quiet** (kwī′ ət)

Sound and Spelling

1. The Long *e* Sound of *ie* as in **yield** and *ei* as in **neither**

The sound of *ie* and *ei* is the same, but the spelling isn't.

ie

Write the words that have the same vowel sound and the same consonant ending as the numbered word.

brief   chief   field   grief   grieves   piece   shield   wield

1. yield   _____   _____   _____

2. niece   _____

3. thief   _____   _____   _____

4. thieves   _____

ei

Read the words.

Only a few short, common words are spelled by *ei*.

either   seize   Neil   Keith

Read some of these words and others that have *ie* and *ei* in sentences.

1. <u>Keith</u> picked up a <u>piece</u> of money the <u>thieves</u> dropped.

2. The <u>chief</u> of traffic control gave a <u>brief</u> account of how my <u>niece</u> failed to <u>yield</u> the right of way to the other car.

3. Riot cops use <u>shields</u> and <u>wield</u> heavy clubs at crowds that are out of control.

4. He broke his father's watch when the <u>thief</u> tried to <u>seize</u> his bag, and he stil' <u>grieves</u> over it.

5. The little boy, dressed up as a mad <u>fiend</u> with claws and sharp teeth, made loud <u>shrieks</u> to frighten us.

Longer, Common *ie* Words with the Long *e* Sound

Write in *ie* and read the words, giving *ie* the long *e* sound you hear in yield.

1. rel __ __ f	4. bel __ __ f	7. d __ __ sel	10. coll __ __
2. rel __ __ ve	5. bel __ __ ve	8. ap __ __ ce	11. br __ __ fcase
3. mov __ __	6. ach __ __ ve	9. brown __ __	12. Mar __ __

Longer, Common *ei* Words with the Long *e* Sound

Write in *ei* and read the words, giving *ei* the long *e* sound you hear in neither.

1. c __ __ ling	3. rec __ __ pt	5. conc __ __ ted	7. Sh __ __ la
2. __ __ ther	4. caff __ __ ne	6. rec __ __ ve	8. dec __ __ ve

2. The Sound of *ei* as in **eight**

Write the words that have the same vowel sound and the same consonant ending as the numbered word.

> *g* and *gh* are silent in these words.

freight   rein   reign   sleigh   weight

1. eight   _____ _____

2. vein   _____ _____

3. weigh   _____

> There aren't many *ei* words

Read these words and others that have the long *a* sound of *ei* in sentences.

1. The beige veil on her hat was more gray than tan.

2. He played Santa, sitting in a sleigh, holding the reins in his hand.

3. The English queen reigns, but what she says carries little weight.

4. Let's weigh the box to find out what the freight charges will be.

5. Blood from a vein is darker than blood coming from an artery.

3. Spelling *ie* and *ei* Words

There is a little "poem" about spelling *ie* and *ei* that is of some help, but it doesn't apply to many words:

> Write *i* before *e*
> But not after *c*
> Or when sounded like *a*
> As in **neighbor** and **weigh**.

Write the words and add *ing*, *ed*, and *s*.

1. weigh   _____, _____, _____

2. yield   _____, _____, _____

3. grieve   _____, _____, _____

4. piece   _____, _____, _____

Write the words and add *er*, *ed*, and *s*.

1. believe   _____, _____, _____

2. deceive   _____, _____, _____

3. receive   _____, _____, _____

Syllables and Accents

1. Writing Words in Syllables

Write the words in syllables and put in the main accents.

1. battlefield   _____ _____ _____

2. calorie   _____ _____ _____

3. neighborly   _____ _____ _____

4. rabies   _____ _____

5. deceitful   _____ _____ _____

6. unveiled   _____ _____

7. disbelief   _____ _____ _____

8. achievement   _____ _____ _____

9. grievance   _____ _____

10. unweighed   _____ _____

2. Split Vowels in *ie* Words

> The sounds are long *i*, short *i*, short *e*, or the schwa.

Write the words in syllables and mark the main accents.

1. diet _____ _____
2. quiet _____ _____
3. client _____ _____
4. pliers _____ _____
5. science _____ _____

6. fiery _____ _____ _____
7. Soviet _____ _____ _____
8. alien _____ _____ _____
9. Vietnam _____ _____ _____
10. Vienna _____ _____ _____

Combine the syllables into a whole word and read it.

1. va ri e ty _____
2. so ci e ty _____
3. anx i e ty _____
4. o ri ent _____
5. o ri en tal _____

6. ex pe ri ence _____
7. o be di ence _____
8. in gre di ent _____
9. re cip i ent _____
10. aud i ence _____

Read some of these words in sentences.

1. A pair of pliers solves a variety of problems if your hands are weak.

2. Judges get experience in dealing with society's problems.

3. The crew suffered from great anxiety after seeing the fiery plane crash.

4. Rich ingredients such as butter and cream are found in the food of Vienna, the capital of Austria.

5. Part of Soviet territory was in the Far East, land of Oriental people.

6. Children of Vietnam are taught obedience at home and at school.

7. The family was a recipient of food stamps and other aid.

Dictionary Marks and Less-Common Words

ie in **yield** (yēld)	*ei* in **neither** (nē′ thər)	*ei* in **eight** (āt)

> When you use the dictionary to spell and pronounce words, you must look down the page for *ie, ei, e, ee, ea, ey* if you hear the long *e* sound. You might also have to look under *i* or *a* if you hear those sounds. It's the same problem when looking for a name in the telephone book.

1. Learning the Markings with Words You Know

Write the word after the respelling.

brief   freight   Keith   Neil   piece
sleigh   seize   shield   vein   weight

1. vān _____
2. shēld _____
3. slā _____
4. nēl _____
5. wāt _____

6. pēs _____
7. sēz _____
8. brēf _____
9. kēth _____
10. frāt _____

2. Writing Less-Common Words

Write the word after the respelling.

aggrieved   besieged   codeine   conceive
perceive   protein   reprieve   surveillance

1. kō′ dēn _____
2. ri prēv′ _____

3. kən sēv′ _____
4. ə grēvd′ _____

5. pro' tēn _____ **7.** pər sēv' _____

6. sər vā' ləns _____ **8.** bi sējd' _____

Read these words in sentences.

1. We felt <u>aggrieved</u> when the jury awarded us only one dollar damages.

2. Every spring we are <u>besieged</u> with big black ants in the kitchen.

3. The dentist gave me <u>codeine</u> to relieve the pain.

4. A good <u>protein</u> source is milk and lentils, as well as meat and fish.

5. I can't <u>conceive</u> why you didn't get a receipt for paying the bill.

6. Anybody could <u>perceive</u> the child was tired and hungry.

7. The doomed convict hoped for a <u>reprieve</u> from the governor.

8. F.B.I. men are watching the house; it is under constant <u>surveillance</u>.

3. Out-of-Pattern and Other Confusing Words

In some out-of-pattern words, *ei* has the long *i* sound as in **height** (hīt). In a few *ie* and *ei* words, you hear short *i* as in **kerchief** (kʉr' chif) and short *e* as in **friend** (frend).

> The sound in **their**, and a few more words, is like the *er* in **very**.

Write the words in the blanks.

counterfeit   Fahrenheit   feisty   foreign   forfeit   Geiger
heifer   heirloom   heist   mischief   sieve   sleight

1. Strain the chicken broth through a _____ (siv).

2. This old garnet necklace is a family _____ (er' loom).

3. Thieves pulled a _____ (hīst) of a money truck but were caught.

4. The brown _____ (hef' ər) isn't old enough to have a calf.

5. They used a _____ (gī' gər) counter to look for radioactive ore.

6. The little dog was so _____ (fī' stē), I didn't dare pet him.

7. We have several people from _____ (fôr' in) lands in our class.

8. If it were 95 degrees _____ (fer' ən hīt'), I would _____ (fôr' fit) the race and be happy to lose.

9. Making _____ (koun' tər fit) money is more than just _____ (mis' chif); it's a felony.

10. We were fooled by the _____ (slīt)-of-hand tricks at the show.

"How Do You Say Your Name?"

Most names with *ie* have the long *e* sound: <u>Fields</u>, <u>Priest</u>, <u>Garfield</u>. Most names with *ei* have the long *i* sound; these are mainly German names: <u>Geiger</u>, <u>Stein</u>, <u>Klein</u>. In a few names, mainly from the British Isles, you hear long *e* even when the *e* comes first: <u>O'Neill</u> and <u>MacNeil</u>. A few names have a split vowel: <u>O'Brien</u> and <u>Sierra</u>.

Remembering what you have just learned in this chapter, practice reading *ie* and *ei* names.

Diesel	Oppenheimer	Gottlieb	Tallchief
Ziegler	Steinmetz	Weissmuller	Friedan
Heilman	Feinstein	Eisenhower	Friedman
Meir	Hammerstein	Wiesel	Steinem

Even after following the rules, don't be surprised if some people correct you in pronouncing their names.

Handling *ie* and *ei* Words . . . Lightly

The Business Pages of the Phone Book

Circle the 9 names of groups engaged in business for profit. The other groups are nonprofit and have the aim of helping people or studying a problem.

Alzheimer's Disease and Related Disorders Group

Den of Thieves

Oriental Foods and Supply

Old Heidelberg Inn

Poultry Science Society

Masonic Relief

Detroit Diesel, Inc.

Neighborhood Watch

Consolidated Freight Ways

A-Plus Dog Obedience School

Eightball Saloon

Friend of the Court

H.J. Heinz Company

The Heights and the Pits

Vietnam Veterans of America

Movie Titles?

8 of the following movie titles never existed. Circle them.

Romeo and Juliet

The Great Ziegfeld

Young Frankenstein

Good Morning, Vietnam

Fiendish Caffeine

Murder on the Orient Express

Wuthering Heights

Surveillance of the Weight Watchers

The Believers

Neighborly Achievement

Protein Place

Foreign Correspondent

To Catch a Thief

High Anxiety

The Quiet Man

The Man on the Eiffel Tower

Falling Ceilings

Fahrenheit 451

The Seventh Veil

Heidi

Diesel Engines

Neither

Poltergeist

Battlefield Heebie-Jeebies

Famous People

<u>Read brief accounts of famous achievers.</u>

Albert Einstein, German-born scientist, was believed by his parents and teachers to be retarded. One teacher told him, unbelievably, to drop out of school because he wouldn't achieve anything. Einstein fled to the United States from the fiendish Hitler. He was honored around the world and received many high awards.

William Leidesdorff, a former slave in the early eighteen hundreds, came to California and got rich. The ingredients for his success were hard work and luck. He was a ship captain, a trader, and a land owner. He hadn't perceived there was gold on the land he bought, but there was. He died at 38, leaving his heirs $1,500,000.

Rod Steiger, actor, has played the parts of a grieving pawnbroker, a feisty Southern cop, a priest, and a deceitful husband. Steiger has experienced three divorces and three heart by-passes. He is a man who must have anxiety problems. But he has found relief in counseling and now helps others with heart trouble.

Barbra Streisand, actress and singer, always wanted to be an actress and not a society wife, as her family wished. Obedience was not what made her a big star. To get relief from the nagging, Streisand took a job in an Oriental restaurant, saved her money, and went to acting school.

Artur Rubinstein, world-famous pianist, drew big audiences even at the age of 89. He couldn't conceive of a meal without wine, and he smoked three cigars a day. He got his protein from eating chicken and fish and many fruits and vegetables. He was thought of as conceited by many, but he was the recipient of great praise and respect.

Chapter 9
The
Vowel y

y as in **cry** (krī)　　　　　*y* as in **gym** (jim)

Sound and Spelling

1. The Sounds of *y* as in **cry** and in **gym**

In most words, *y* is a vowel. As a vowel, *y* is a substitute for *i*.

The Long *i* Sound of *y*

Write in *y* and read the words.

One word has a silent *h*.

b __　cr __　dr __　H __　L __le　pl __　pr __　rh __me
sh __　sk __　sl __　spr __　st __le　tr __　t __pe

Read sentences with some of these words and others with *y* as the vowel.

1. Lyle is a man with style, and for a man of ninety, he is very spry.

2. My table is made from a five-ply board.

3. The words fly, fry, and why all rhyme.

4. Hy's place is as dirty as a pig sty.

The Short *i* Sound of *y* as in **gym**

Write the words in the blanks and put in *y* instead of the darkened letter *i*.

> In these words, *i* has replaced *y* ONLY to show how one vowel can take the place of the other. The word you are going to write is the standard way it is spelled. One word has a silent *h*.

1. gim   _gym_
2. himn   _____
3. rhithm _____
4. Linn   _____
5. linx   _____

6. gip   _____
7. cist   _____
8. linch _____
9. cript _____
10. mith _____

Read these words in sentences.

1. Lynn worked out at the women's gym.

2. The hymn we sang in church had the rhythm of old-time gospel music.

3. Because of his ear tufts, my cat looks like a lynx.

4. The dog had a cyst growing on its tail.

5. When a crowd takes the law into its own hands, you have a lynch mob.

6. The body was placed in the marble family crypt.

7. She said getting no refund on her ticket was a big gyp.

8. The boy's older sister told him Santa Claus was just a myth.

102

Longer, Common *y* Words

Write in *y* and put the long vowel mark over the 6 *y* words with the long *i* sound.

1. n __ lon
2. s __ rup __
3. h __ giene

4. s __ mptom
5. c __ clist
6. S __ dney

7. pl __ wood
8. satisf __
9. t __ pist

10. cr __ stal
11. s __ stem
12. bic __ cle

2. Spelling *y* Words

Write the words and add *ing*, *ed* and *es*.

> ☞ *Remember:* Change *y* to *i* when adding *ed*, and *es*, and *ance*.

1. cry _____, _____, _____
2. try _____, _____, _____
3. apply _____, _____, _____
4. rely _____, _____, _____

Write the words and add *ance*.

1. rely _____
2. defy _____

3. ally _____
4. apply _____

Read some of these words in sentences.

1. He applied for a job selling TV sets at the Home Appliance store.

2. We put too much reliance on doctors for good health.

3. Was she fired because of her defiance of company rules?

4. The farmers and workers formed an alliance for passage of better laws.

Syllables and Accents

1. Writing Words in Syllables

Write the words in syllables and put in the main accent.

1. dynamite _____ _____ _____
2. paralyze _____ _____ _____
3. sympathy _____ _____ _____
4. mystery _____ _____ _____
5. Carolyn _____ _____ _____
6. cylinder _____ _____ _____
7. recycle _____ _____ _____
8. cyclist _____ _____
9. gymnastics _____ _____ _____
10. amethyst _____ _____ _____
11. Marilyn _____ _____ _____
12. hypodermic _____ _____ _____ _____

Read these words in sentences.

1. We use <u>cylinders</u> daily: paper tubes, engine parts, drains, and pipes.

2. The <u>cyclist</u> was lucky that his fall in the bike race didn't <u>paralyze</u> him.

3. <u>Carolyn</u> kept looking for her lost <u>amethyst</u> ring and so didn't get much exercise in her <u>gymnastics</u> class.

4. I have <u>sympathy</u> with the drug addicts who use each other's <u>hypodermic</u> needles, because they could get fatal diseases.

5. <u>Marilyn</u> says we should <u>recycle</u> trash to save space in the dumps.

6. It was a <u>mystery</u> why the <u>dynamite</u> didn't blow up the whole building.

2. The Shifted Accent

Write the second word in syllables and put in the main accent mark.

1. sys′ tem   systematic   *sys   tem   at′   ic*
2. dy′ na mite   dynamic   _____ _____ _____
3. ap ply′   applicant   _____ _____ _____
4. symp′ tom   symptomatic   _____ _____ _____ _____
5. par′ a lyze   paralysis   _____ _____ _____ _____
6. spec′ i fy   specific   _____ _____ _____

Read these words in sentences.

1. The computer <u>system</u> makes banking even more <u>systematic</u>.

2. <u>Dynamite</u> can move bridges; a <u>dynamic</u> speaker can move people to act.

3. I was the only <u>applicant</u> to <u>apply</u> for the job in the newspaper ad.

4. Of all the <u>symptoms</u>, fever is the most <u>symptomatic</u> of illness.

5. A stroke often causes <u>paralysis</u>, but it may not <u>paralyze</u> the whole body.

6. When you <u>specify</u> what repairs are needed, be <u>specific</u> about details.

3. Word Building

Put a slash between the syllables and put in the main accent marks. Read the words in sentences.

1. **sympathy   sympathize   sympathetic   sympathetically**

   If you feel <u>sympathy</u> with the poor, you are a <u>sympathetic</u> person. I <u>sympathize</u> with the refugees. He treated his students <u>sympathetically</u>.

2. **mystery   mysterious   mysteriously   mysteriousness**

   It is not so <u>mysterious</u> that the boy loves reading <u>mystery</u> stories. The rash went away as <u>mysteriously</u> as it appeared. I was annoyed with all her <u>mysteriousness</u>.

3. **analyze   analyst   analysis   analytical**

The doctor's assistant will <u>analyze</u> the blood samples. She went to the mental health clinic to be treated by an <u>analyst</u>. An <u>analysis</u> of the blood was done in the lab. Doctors must be trained in <u>analytical</u> thinking to make the right diagnosis.

4. **hygiene   hygienist   hygienic   hygienically**

Eating good food is important for good <u>hygiene</u>. My dental <u>hygienist</u> told me to use dental floss daily. Getting enough sleep regularly is good <u>hygienic</u> practice. The whole flooded area was <u>hygienically</u> unsafe.

5. **hypnosis   hypnotize   hypnotist   hypnotism**

She was allergic to anesthetics, so the dentist tried <u>hypnosis</u> on her before pulling the tooth. If your mind isn't in the right state, nobody can <u>hypnotize</u> you. People should be trained as <u>hypnotists</u> before they practice <u>hypnotism</u>. He thought <u>hypnotism</u> would help him quit smoking.

4. Split Vowels

ia

Write the words in syllables.

1. Sylvia _____ _____
   _____

2. Cynthia _____ _____
   _____

3. hysteria _____ _____ _____
   _____

4. dyslexia _____ _____
   _____ _____

5. Syria _____ _____
   _____

6. encyclopedia _____ _____
   _____ _____
   _____ _____

Read these words in sentences.

1. <u>Sylvia</u> and <u>Cynthia</u> are two of my favorite names for a woman.

2. The child's crying was so close to <u>hysteria</u> that we couldn't calm him.

3. If you reverse letters when you read, your problem may be <u>dyslexia</u>.

4. Most of the people of <u>Syria</u>, a country of the Middle East, are Arabic.

5. You can learn the facts about almost anything in a good <u>encyclopedia</u>.

ya, yo, ye, iu

Write the words in syllables.

1. Wyoming _____ _____ _____

2. Tokyo _____ _____ _____

3. Hyatt _____ _____

4. cyanide _____ _____ _____

5. polyester _____ _____ _____ _____

6. gymnasium _____ _____ _____ _____

Read these words in sentences.

1. Yellowstone Park is in <u>Wyoming</u>, a northwestern state.

2. There is a <u>Hyatt</u> Hotel in <u>Tokyo</u>, Japan's largest city.

3. <u>Cyanide</u>, a deadly poison, smells of bitter almond.

4. Unlike cotton and wool, <u>polyester</u> is a man-made fabric.

5. They don't play basketball in the old <u>gymnasium</u> now.

Dictionary Marks and Less-Common Words

> **cry** (krī)   **gym** (jim)

Words with **y** as a vowel are respelled like **i** words. Many dictionaries, however, respell the final **y** as an **e** sound when the y is short: **funny** (fun′ē), **silly** (sil′ē). The two sounds are very close.

1. Learning the Markings with Words You Know

Write the words after the respelling. Try to spell the words without looking at the list.

dry   hymn   Lynn   my   spry   style

1. mī _____
2. him _____
3. lin _____
4. drī _____
5. sprī _____
6. stīl _____

2. Writing Less-Common Words

Write the words after the respellings.

enzyme   hysterics   larynx   onyx   polyp   pylon
Pyrex   stylus   syringe   thyroid   tyrant   vinyl

1. tī′rənt _____
2. his ter′iks _____
3. pī′reks _____
4. en′zīm _____
5. thī′roid _____
6. stī′ləs _____
7. pol′ip _____
8. lar′iŋks _____
9. sə rinj′ _____
10. on′iks _____
11. vī′n′l _____
12. pī′lon _____

Read these words in sentences.

1. Soap with <u>enzymes</u> will fade the stains in this shirt.

2. The vocal cords are in the <u>larynx</u>.

108

3. The onyx stone in her ring has layers of lovely colors.

4. A polyp growing on the vocal cords can cause trouble with speaking.

5. The worker climbed the pylon to repair the wires and transformers.

6. A Pyrex baking dish can go from the freezer right into the oven.

7. Some children had hysterics when they saw the crash.

8. Marilyn used a stylus to cut her license number on her TV set.

9. No syringe should be reused, since blood carries diseases.

10. The thyroid gland in the front of the neck controls growth.

11. Everyone in the family must do as the father says; he is a tyrant.

12. These old jazz records are not made of vinyl and break easily.

Write the words in the blanks.

anonymous	asylum	dynasty	homonyms	hydrogen	polygamy
pyramids	sycamore	symbolic	synagogue	synonym	synthetic

1. The huge, desert _____ (pir′ ə mids) were tombs for kings.

2. Some _____ (sin thet′ ik) leather looks like the real thing.

3. The English royal family comes from an old _____
(dī′ nəs tē).

4. The man was married to three wives at the same time; he was guilty of
_____ (pə lig′ ə mē).

5. A mental hospital used to be called an _____ (ə sī′ ləm).

6. I know by the handwriting who wrote this _____
(ə non′ ə məs) note.

7. The gas _____ (hī′ drə jən) has no odor or color.

8. The holy building of the Jews is called a _____ (sin′ ə gog′).

9. Pair and **pear** are _____ (hom′ ə nims) because they sound the same, but they are spelled differently and have a different meaning.

10. Collect is a _____ (sin′ ə nim) for **gather**; the two words have the same meaning.

11. You can spot a _____ (sik′ ə môr′) tree by its flaky bark.

12. Saluting the flag is _____ (sim bol′ ik) of respect for one's country.

3. Out-of-Pattern and Other Confusing Words.

☆ When adding **ing** to **dye** (to color) you keep the final **e**: **dyeing**. In **die** (to stop living), change **i** to **y** and drop **e** when adding **ing**: **dying**. This is also true of **tie — tying**.

☆ Most dictionaries show both **flier** or **flyer, frier** or **fryer, drier** or **dryer**. Either is an acceptable spelling.

"How Do You Say Your Name?"

You can use the syllable rules for pronouncing names, but some names still leave you uncertain, as do common words with only one consonant between two vowels.

Read and cross out the names that leave you in doubt about pronouncing them.

Dylan	Ryder	Pryor	MacGyver
Dykstra	Van Dyke	Carlyle	Stanwyck
Hyster	Wyatt	Allyson	Hysen
Blythe	Spyro Gyra	Brynner	Forsythe
Joslyn	Bryson	Kyser	Lynyrd Skynyrd

Handling *y* Words . . . Lightly

Confusing Business Names

An employment office may send you to a company you have never heard of. You can now pronounce these unusual (and often made-up) names, but you may wonder what the company does to earn its money. Circle the names that would puzzle most people outside the business.

General Dynamics Hydroflo Systems Hyatt Legal Services

Cycle Cellar Symbolics, Inc. Body Works Gym

Hygienetics Pyramid Office Supply Cybertronics

Envirodyne Engineers House of Styles Teledyne

Gifts-N-Tyme Flying Fingers Typing Industrial Analysts

Olympic Motel Cytrix Corp. Rosslyn Apartments

Colortyme Paint Co. Lytton Industries Unisys

Odd Word Out

Cross out the word that doesn't belong, and then write the name of the group (or category) in the blank.

ailments   animals   cleaning products   female names   jobs
male names   man-made   music   places   plants
                materials

1. Cynthia, Gwendolyn, Meryl, Marilyn, Gladys, Clyde, Sybil, Sylvia
   _____

2. typist, dental hygienist, tyrant, Presbyterian minister, gym teacher, mystery writer _____

3. sycamore, cyprus, water hyacinth, crystal, lily, creeping myrtle
   _____

4. Cyril, Darryl, Sylvester, Lyndon, Cyrus, Tyrone, Kathryn
   _____

5. amethysts, nylon, acrylic, vinyl, polyester, styrofoam _____

6. paralysis, laryngitis, cystic fibrosis, Wyoming, polyp _____

7. lynx, gypsy moth, python, myna bird, Senator Byrd, hyena
   _____

8. Oxydol, Ty-D-Bol, Log Cabin Syrup, Lysol, Dyna-Kleen _____

9. rhythm, lyrics, symptoms, calypso, cymbals, hymns _____

10. Egypt, Syria, Brooklyn, Syracuse, Tylenol, Libya, Gettysburg
    _____

Problem Solving

In some telephone books, groups and establishments whose purposes are to offer help in solving a problem are listed separately from businesses. Circle the 6 names you would find in a listing of nonprofit helping groups.

Alliance for the Mentally Ill

Sudden Infant Death
   Syndrome

Encyclopedia Americana

Lyme Disease Support Group

Gamblers Anonymous
   Support Group

Adult Dyslexic Group

Dynamic Tutoring

Dy-Dee Service

Parents Anonymous

Lifestyle Fitness

Merwyn's Department Store

Sources of City and Village Names

Write **n** after nature names or **p** after people (family or first) names. One name is neither from nature nor a person's name. Don't mark it.

Butterfly	Cyprus Gardens	Gettysburg	Rye
Onyx	Ypsilanti	Dyersburg	Tyler
Holly Hills	Sylvester	Gypsum	Lynchburg
Wytheville	Bryan	Myers Corners	Cynthiana
Fordyce	Tysons Corner	Tyrone	Sin Deny

Music: Groups or Single Performers

Circle the single performers.

Bob Dylan	The System
Crystal Gayle	The Sex Cymbals
Alyson Williams	The Hypocrites
Loretta Lynn	Dynamite Twins
The Abyss	Cyndi Lauper
Leontyne Price	Jessye Norman
Calypso Season	Lynyrd Skynyrd

Chapter 10
ph and *ch*

---

ph as in **phone** (fōn)   *ch* as in **school** (skōol)
ch as in **Michigan** (mish′ ə gən)

Sound and Spelling

1. The Sound of *ph* as in **phone**

The letters *ph* almost always spell the sound of *f*.

Rewrite the words and put *ph* in place of the darkened letter *f*.

In this exercise, *f* has been used to replace *ph* ONLY to show how one sound is spelled in another way. In these words, *ph*, instead of *f*, is the standard spelling, the way you will write them. People's names, however, are often spelled in different ways.

1. Josef   *Joseph*   7. orfan _____

2. Filip _____   8. Fyllis _____

3. nefew _____   9. Randolf _____

4. trofy _____   10. Rudolf _____

5. Memfis _____   11. fony _____

6. asfalt _____   12. Sofie _____

Read these words in sentences.

1. My <u>nephew</u> <u>Rudolph</u> won the <u>trophy</u> for long-distance running.

2. <u>Phyllis</u> and her twin brother, <u>Philip</u>, were born in <u>Memphis</u>, Tennessee.

3. Snow melts quickly on a black <u>asphalt</u> driveway.

4. <u>Sophie</u> is not an <u>orphan</u>; both her parents are still alive.

5. <u>Joseph</u> says <u>Randolph</u> is telling the truth, but he sounds so <u>phony</u>.

Longer, Common Words with *ph*

Write *ph* in the blanks and read the word.

1. ele __ __ ant

2. al __ __ abet

3. ty __ __ oid

4. autogra __ __

5. __ __ onogra __ __

6. __ __ otogra __ __

7. so __ __ omore

8. saxo __ __ one

9. __ __ ysical

2. The Sound of *ch* as in **school**

In some words, *ch* spells the *k* sound. In reading *ch* words, first try the most common sound, *ch* as in **chip**, and then try the *k* sound heard in **school**.

Rewrite the word and put *ch* in place of the darkened letter *k*.

In this exercise, *k* has been used to replace *ch* ONLY to show how one sound is spelled in another way. The standard spelling, which you will write, is with *ch*. People's names are not always spelled the same way.

1. skool _____ 4. ake _____

2. Kris _____ 5. krome _____

3. Krist _____ 6. skeme _____

Longer, Common Words with the *k* Sound of *ch*

Write *ch* in the blanks and read the words, giving *ch* the *k* sound.

1. stoma __ __   4. __ __ orus   7. __ __ rysler

2. an __ __ or   5. Mi __ __ ael   8. __ __ ristmas

3. e __ __ o   6. s __ __ edule   9. me __ __ anic

3. The Sound of *ch* as in **chef**

In a few words, *ch* has the soft sound of *sh* as in **ship**. The sounds
are close to the sound of *ch* as in **chip**.

Rewrite the word and put *ch* in place of the darkened letters *sh*.

> In this exercise, *sh* has been used to
> replace *ch* ONLY to show how one
> sound is spelled in another way. The
> standard spelling, which you will
> write, is with *ch*. One word has a
> silent *g*.

1. **sh**ampagne _____ 5. para**sh**ute _____

2. **Sh**icago _____   6. musta**sh**e _____

3. **Sh**arlotte _____ 7. **sh**andelier _____

4. Mi**sh**igan _____   8. **sh**iffon _____

4. Spelling *ph* and *ch* Words

You may have to look in the *f*, as well as the *ph*, parts of the dictionary and phone book. And, of course, in spelling *ch* words, you may also have to look in the *c, k,* and *sh* parts of the dictionary, as well as in the *ch* part.

Write the words and add *ing, ed,* and *s*.

1. phone _____, _____, _____

2. schedule _____, _____, _____

3. photograph _____, _____, _____

4. ache _____, _____, _____

Write the words and add *s* or *es*.

1. chorus _____

2. phonograph _____

3. trophy _____

Syllables and Accents

ph and *ch* are not split in almost all words.

1. Writing Words in Syllables

Write the words in syllables and put in the main accents.

1. orchestra _____ _____ _____

2. pharmacy _____ _____ _____

3. chemistry _____ _____ _____

4. character _____ _____ _____

5. scholarship   _____ _____ _____

6. pre-Christmas   _____ _____ _____

7. symphony   _____ _____ _____

8. atmosphere   _____ _____ _____

9. phoniness   _____ _____ _____

10. stenographer   _____ _____ _____ _____

11. syphilis   _____ _____ _____

12. nonphysical   _____ _____ _____ _____

13. emphasize   _____ _____ _____

14. technical   _____ _____ _____

2. Writing Related Words

Write the words in the blanks after the related word and put in the main accent marks.

      atmospheric   characteristics   choral   pharmacist   scholastic

1. chorus   _____

2. character   _____

3. atmosphere   _____

4. scholarship   _____

5. pharmacy   _____

3. Reading *ph* and *ch* Words

Read some of the words in sections 1 and 2 in sentences.

1. The school's <u>chorus</u> director wanted the <u>symphony</u> <u>orchestra</u> to play more <u>choral</u> music, so that his people could perform with them.

2. To win a <u>scholarship</u> for college, he had to keep his <u>scholastic</u> average up.

3. It was <u>characteristic</u> of that good man to be <u>nonphysical</u> in correcting his children.

4. The power plant was pouring lethal smoke into the <u>atmosphere</u>.

5. A tornado, with its turbulent air, might be called an <u>atmospheric</u> disaster.

6. The army doctors give classes on how to prevent <u>syphilis</u>.

4. Word Building

Mark the syllables with slashes and put in the main accent. Read the words in sentences.

1. **alphabet   alphabetize   alphabetical   alphabetically**

   The letter **m** is in the middle of the <u>alphabet</u>. Someone did not <u>alphabetize</u> these cards right. Please put the names in <u>alphabetical</u> order. We were seated <u>alphabetically</u>.

2. **emphasize   emphasis   emphatic**

   I must <u>emphasize</u> how important it is to be on time on this job. The family put <u>emphasis</u> on good manners and reading. The boss was <u>emphatic</u> about when the job had to be finished.

3. **photograph   photography   photographer**

   He gave me a <u>photograph</u> of himself. The book on <u>photography</u> came with the new camera. She was a <u>photographer</u> of children and pets.

4. **chemist   chemicals   chemistry   chemotherapy**

   A <u>chemist</u> must handle acid with great care. Detergents are made by mixing <u>chemicals</u>. A <u>chemistry</u> lab often smells of rotten eggs. The doctor ordered <u>chemotherapy</u> for treating the cancer.

5. mechanic   mechanical   mechanize

Phil is a good mechanic on any make of car. The plane had mechanical problems that grounded it. When the company began to mechanize the plant, many workers were laid off.

6. technical   technology   technicality

The space ship had a technical problem and was grounded. In our age of computers and other high technology, we have to read many difficult words. The accused man was let off on a technicality of the law, but we felt he was guilty.

5. Split Vowels in *ph* and *ch* Words

Write *f* over *ph* and *k* over *ch*. Then write the words in syllables.

> You will split *ia, eo, io, ea,* and *ao*.
> Look for silent *p* and *g*.

1. geography   *ge ̶ og ̶ ra ̶ phy*
2. biography _____ _____ _____
3. Philadelphia _____ _____ _____ _____
4. psychiatrist _____ _____ _____
5. diaphragm _____ _____ _____
6. chaos _____ _____
7. trachea _____ _____ _____
8. diphtheria _____ _____ _____

Read these words in sentences.

1. Ralph learned about Michigan and other places in geography class.

2. Lincoln's life is well-known, but another biography of him is just out.

3. Michael lived in Philadelphia, one of the biggest cities on the East coast.

4. Your diaphragm is your midriff, between the chest and abdomen.

5. Phyllis was so upset by the wreck that she was seeing a <u>psychiatrist</u>.

6. When the teacher left the room, there was disorder, total <u>chaos</u>.

7. Meat became stuck in Charlotte's <u>trachea</u>, and she almost choked.

8. The baby was given shots for whooping cough and <u>diphtheria</u>.

Dictionary Marks and Less-Common Words

> *ph* as in **phone** (fōn), *ch* as in **school** (skōōl), and *ch* as in **Michigan** (mish′ ə gən)

Dictionaries respell *ph* with *f*. They respell some *ch* words with *k* and others with *sh*.

1. Learning the Markings with Words You Know

Write the words after the respellings. Try to write the words without looking at the list.

ache	asphalt	Chris	Christ	chrome	Joseph	nephew
orphan	Philip	photo	Ralph	scheme		

1. jō′ zəf _____
2. nef′ yōō _____
3. kris _____
4. ôr′ fən _____
5. skēm _____
6. āk _____

7. fil′ əp _____
8. fō′ tō _____
9. krōm _____
10. ralf _____
11. krīst _____
12. as′ fôlt _____

2. Writing Less-Common Words
ph (*f*) as in **phone**

Write the words in the blank.

dolphin   emphysema   esophagus   graphics   hemisphere   hyphens
paragraph   phonics   phosphates   physics   sapphire   siphon

1. The _____ (dol′ fən) is related to the whale.

2. You will study energy in _____ (fiz′ iks) class.

3. You know _____ (fon′ iks), the sound of letters and syllables.

4. Most farmers use fertilizer with _____ (fos′ fāts) in them.

5. We enjoyed learning to draw in _____ (graf′ iks) class.

6. Our Western _____ (hem′ ə sfir′) is half of the world.

7. If food gets stuck in the _____ (i sof′ ə gəs), you choke.

8. She loved rubies and the blue, expensive _____ (saf′ īr).

9. The words in *free-for-all* are joined by _____ (hī′ fəns).

10. May I _____ (sī′ fən) out a gallon of gas from your car?

11. When the air sacs in the lungs don't stretch, you have _____ (em′ fə sē′ mə) and may need an oxygen tank to breathe.

12. A new _____ (par′ ə graf′) means another idea, and you must move the first line in a few spaces.

123

ch (*k*) as in **school**

Write the words after the respellings.

architect   bronchitis   chiropractor   chloride   chloroform   cholesterol

chromosomes   cholera   chronic   monarch   psychology   strychnine

1. kol′ ər ə   _____

2. klôr′ īd   _____

3. kī′ rə prak′ tər _____

4. sī kol′ ə jē   _____

5. är′ kə tekt′   _____

6. klôr′ ə fôrm′   _____

7. mon′ ərk   _____

8. krō′ mə sōms′ _____

9. kron′ ik   _____

10. strik′ nīn   _____

11. kə les′ tə rol′   _____

12. bron kit′ is   _____

Read these words in sentences.

1. Drinking infected water can bring on cholera, a disease causing vomiting.

2. His back pain was always there; it was chronic.

3. This psychology book may explain why he misbehaved.

4. Stray dogs were being killed by strychnine poison.

5. Queen Elizabeth is the monarch of England.

6. The mechanic's back was helped by a chiropractor.

7. Common table salt is sodium chloride.

8. The school's architect planned a separate wing for the shops.

9. A bad cough often comes with bronchitis.

10. We had the sick dog sniff chloroform to put it out of its misery.

11. The parents' chromosomes shape the baby.

12. Eating butter may raise the cholesterol level of the blood.

ch (*sh*) as in **Michigan**

Write the words after the respellings.

champagne　　chandelier　　chaperone　　echelon　　parachute　　pistachio

1. pi stä′ she o _____

2. par′ ə shoot _____

3. esh′ ə lon′ _____

4. shap′ ə ron _____

5. sham pān′ _____

6. shan′ də lir′ _____

Read these words in sentences.

1. They drank champagne and ate pistachio-nut ice cream at the party.

2. The parent chaperones at the school dance had to break up a fight.

3. A big crystal chandelier lighted every corner of the hotel lobby.

4. When planes fly in a close echelon, it isn't safe to do a parachute jump.

''How Do You Say and Spell Your Name?''

Two of the *ch* sounds are so close that people wouldn't notice if you didn't say the name exactly "right." Chapin (*ch* or *sh*?), Chalmers (*ch* or *sh*?). But names that have the *k* sound of *ch* present a problem, and you often have to ask if you haven't heard the name before or it isn't like a word you already know. The combination *sch* ordinarily has the sound of *sh* as when used in Schmidt.

Circle the famous names that would cause you to ask about spelling and pronouncing.

Humphrey	Christie	Orbach	McPherson	Chamberlain
Chrysler	Pharr	Murdoch	Randolph	Dietrich
Buchanan	Alphonso IV	Christensen	Cochran	Koch
Schell	Phelps	Reichert	Gottschalk	Christoff
Chaplin	Stephens	Philbrick	Echols	Cher

Handling *ph* and *ch* Words . . . Lightly

Books, Light Entertainment?

Some books are just for relaxing and enjoying the story. Other books are mainly for information and require a slower reading rate and a pause now and then to reread a passage. Circle the books that are probably read just for enjoyment.

Phantom Cowboy

Backache Relief

The Seven Sapphires of Mardi Gras

Eddie Murphy's Funny Stories

Moonlight Charade

The Triumph of Love

Who Wears Blue Chiffon, Anyway?

Count Out Cholesterol Cookbook

Parachutes and Kisses

Cher: Forever Fit

The Chronicle of a Funny Man

The Mystery of Phoenix

The Life of President James Buchanan

The People's Pharmacy

The Autobiography of Malcolm X

Agatha Christie's murder mysteries

Graphics: Turbo C++

The Trophy

History of Philosophy

Scoring to Win in a Chaotic World

Echoes from Her Past

The Chicago Loop Murder

Zachary Taylor's War

How to Grow Giant Chrysanthemums

Ailments

Circle the 12 problems one would see a doctor about.

stomach ulcers

syphilis

paragraph rules

bronchitis

character weaknesses

hydrophobia shots

chronic headache

chandeliers

diphtheria

emphysema

phobias about high places

sophomore grades

asphalt paving

typhoid fever

pistachio nuts

allergies to chemicals

choosing a good chiropractor

melancholic, blue feelings

Odd Word Out

Circle the word that does not belong in the group and write the name of the category in the blank.

animals   chemicals   jobs   music   reading and writing

1. paragraphs, apostrophes, alphabet, atmosphere, phonics, pamphlets, hyphens, phrases _____

2. pheasants, gophers, chameleons, dolphins, aphids, elephants, photographs _____

3. stenographers, chemists, pharmacists, Chevrolets, geographers, mechanics, choral directors, psychologists, chauffeurs _____

4. orchestra, symphony, chord, philharmonic, parachute, chorus

   _____

5. phosphorus, chloroform, emphasis, sulphuric acid, hydrochloric acid, chlorophyl, camphor _____

New Company Names

Circle the 9 company names that were made by shortening one or two words.

Chemlawn	Cholestech	Get Physical	Master Mechanics
Golden Chef	Techrep	Graphink	Green Schemes
Dynatech	The Health Pharm	Synchron	Bechtel Power Corp
Elephant Moving	Acoustech	Chemtreat	Allphase Builder

School District Names

School districts are getting bigger as small places join bigger cities or towns for money reasons. Circle the names you would be surprised to see on a school bus.

Chicago   Memphis   Orphan's Gift   Charlotte

White Elephant   Pumphrey   Phoenix   Philadelphia

Ephrata   Zephyrville   Cheboygan   Jericho

Scholastica   New Rochelle   Olyphant   Anchorage

Chapter 11
More Spellings
of the
sh Sound

ci as in
special (spesh′ əl)
ancient (ān′ shənt)
spacious (spā′ shəs)

ti as in
partial (par′ shəl)
patient (pā′ shənt)
cautious (kô′ shəs)
mention (men′ shən)

si as in **mission** (mish′ ən)

Sound and Spelling

ti, si, and *ci* before another vowel will produce the *sh* sound.

1. The *cia* and *tia* Spelling of the *sh* Sound, as in **special** and **partial**

Write the word putting in *ci* and *ti* instead of the darkened letters *sh*.

> The letters *sh* have been used in this and the next three exercises ONLY to show that *ci, si,* and *ti*, in some words, spell the *sh* sound. The woman's name (in the first group of words) is often spelled with *sh*.

Write in *ci*

1. spe*sh*al   *special*
2. fa*sh*al _____
3. ra*sh*al _____
4. so*sh*al _____
5. Mar*sh*a _____

Write in *ti*

6. par*sh*al _____
7. mar*sh*al _____
8. ini*sh*al _____
9. pala*sh*al _____
10. essen*sh*al _____

Read these words in sentences.

1. The White House is not <u>palatial</u>, but it's fine enough for big <u>social</u> events.

2. <u>Marcia</u> had a mud-pack <u>facial</u>, hoping to lose her wrinkles.

3. The boss writes his <u>initials</u> in a <u>special</u> way on work orders.

4. A <u>racial</u> problem arose because one teacher was <u>partial</u> to one race.

5. After the terrible flood, it was <u>essential</u> to have <u>martial</u> law, though we didn't like having troops controlling our town.

2.   The *cie* and *tie* Spelling of the *sh* Sound, as in **ancient** and **patient**

Write the word putting in *ci* instead of the darkened letters, *sh*.

1. an*sh*ent   _____
2. defi*sh*ent   _____
3. effi*sh*ent   _____

130

4. suffi**sh**ent　　　_____

5. cons**sh**ence　　　_____

Write the words and put in *ti* instead of the darkened letters, *sh*.

1. pa**sh**ent　　　_____

2. pa**sh**ence　　　_____

Read these words in sentences.

1. It's not easy for doctors to have <u>patience</u> with every <u>patient</u> they see.

2. We studied only the Romans and Greeks in <u>ancient</u> history class.

3. If your diet is <u>deficient</u> in iron, eat more liver.

4. The new auto plants are more <u>efficient</u> in saving time and materials.

5. I had <u>sufficient</u> money to help them, and because I didn't do it, I have a bad <u>conscience</u>.

3. The *tion* and *sion* Spelling of the *sh* Sound, as in **mention** and **mission**

Write the word putting in *ti* and *si* instead of the darkened letters, *sh*.

Write in *ti*

1. ac**sh**on　　_____

2. func**sh**on　　_____

3. por**sh**on　　_____

Write in *si*

1. ses**sh**on　　_____

2. pen**sh**on　　_____

3. ten**sh**on　　_____

Read these words in sentences.

1. I needed to take <u>action</u> immediately, but I was sick and couldn't <u>function</u>.

2. The little girl cried because her <u>portion</u> of cake was too small.

3. One <u>session</u> of the meetings was on increasing workers' <u>pensions</u>.

4. There was always <u>tension</u> over money in that family.

4. The *tious* and *cious* Spelling of the *sh* Sound, as in **cautious** and **spacious**

Write the word putting in *ti* and *ci* instead of the darkened letters, *sh*.

Write in *ti*	Write in *ci*
1. cau*sh*ous _____	1. spa*sh*ous _____
2. nutri*sh*ous _____	2. cons*sh*ous _____
3. flirta*sh*ous _____	3. suspi*sh*ous _____

Read these words in sentences.

1. He was very <u>cautious</u> about spending even a dollar.

2. Fruit and vegetables are part of a <u>nutritious</u> diet.

3. The <u>flirtatious</u> young man patted women on the shoulder.

4. The back seat of our car is not <u>spacious</u> enough for his long legs.

5. After she fell, she was barely <u>conscious</u> of what was going on.

6. His wife was so <u>suspicious</u> she went through his pockets nightly.

132

5. Spelling Words with Common Suffixes/Endings with the **sh** Sound

> You must frequently check with the dictionary when spelling words with the **sh** sound.

Write the words and add *ing* and *ed*.

1. mention   _____, _____

2. caution   _____, _____

3. function   _____, _____

4. station   _____, _____

Write the words and add *ly*.

1. racial _____
2. social _____
3. patient _____
4. essential _____

5. efficient _____
6. conscious _____
7. nutritious _____
8. suspicious _____

Syllables and Accents

These syllables, *tial, cial, tian, cian, tien, cien, tion, sion, cious, tious*, are suffixes/endings, and they are not accented.

1. Writing Words in Syllables

Write the syllables in the blanks and put in the main accent mark.

1. commercial   _____ _____ _____

2. presidential   _____ _____ _____ _____

3. completion   _____ _____ _____

4. delicious _____ _____ _____

5. superstitious _____ _____ _____ _____

6. discrimination _____ _____ _____ _____ _____

7. institution _____ _____ _____ _____

8. promotion _____ _____ _____

2. Writing Words in Syllables that Have Prefixes/Beginnings
and Suffixes/Endings

Write the words with prefixes/beginnings and suffixes/endings in syllables.

1. socialize _____ _____ _____

2. nonracial _____ _____ _____

3. especially _____ _____ _____ _____

4. impartial _____ _____ _____

5. unconscious _____ _____ _____

6. specialist _____ _____ _____

7. inefficient _____ _____ _____ _____

8. insufficient _____ _____ _____ _____

9. impatient _____ _____ _____

10. antisocial _____ _____ _____ _____

11. conditional _____ _____ _____ _____

12. missionary _____ _____ _____ _____

3. Matching Related Words

tia and *cia* Words

Match the related words and put in the main accent marks.

> Notice the shifted accents in the words you write.

beneficial	credentials	electrician	financial	judicial	magician
militia	musician	official	politician	residential	substantial

1. music _____
2. magic _____
3. office _____
4. judge _____
5. credit _____
6. finance _____

7. politics _____
8. residence _____
9. military _____
10. electric _____
11. benefit _____
12. substance _____

Read these words in sentences.

1. The rock <u>musician</u> needed an <u>electrician</u> to set up his equipment.

2. The <u>politician</u> asked for an <u>official</u> count of the votes.

3. Finally, the governor called out the <u>militia</u> to control the riot.

4. Magic tricks couldn't solve the <u>magician's</u> <u>financial</u> problems.

5. Living in a safe <u>residential</u> neighborhood is <u>beneficial</u> to your health.

6. Marcia lost a <u>substantial</u> amount of money and was very worried.

7. All courts are in the <u>judicial</u> branch of the government.

8. They asked for my <u>credentials</u>, and I showed my driver's license.

135

tion and *sion* Words

Match the related words and put in the main accent marks.

In some of these words, the accents do not shift when a suffix is added.

admission   execution   expansion   impression   information
invitation   occupation   possession   proposition   resignation

1. admit _____
2. resign _____
3. invite _____
4. inform _____
5. expand _____

6. execute _____
7. occupy _____
8. possess _____
9. propose _____
10. impress _____

4.   Split Vowels

cia, tia, ia, cie

Write the words in syllables and put in the main accent marks.

1. appreciate _____ _____ _____ _____
2. associate _____ _____ _____ _____
3. initiate _____ _____ _____ _____
4. officiate _____ _____ _____ _____
5. negotiate _____ _____ _____ _____
6. pediatrician _____ _____ _____ _____ _____
7. conscientious _____ _____ _____ _____
8. beneficiary _____ _____ _____ _____ _____
_____

Read these words in sentences.

1. I appreciate having the chance to associate with such kind people.

2. The Masonic lodge will initiate new members at the meeting.

136

3. His father, a preacher, will <u>officiate</u> at the wedding.

4. Next fall the committee will <u>negotiate</u> a new contract with GM.

5. The baby's <u>pediatrician</u> gave him some medicine for the fever.

6. A good worker is <u>conscientious</u> about getting to work on time.

7. The child was named <u>beneficiary</u> of his father's policy.

ea, io, and *ia* in *tion* and *sion* Words

Write the words in syllables and put in the main accent marks.

1. creation _____ _____ _____

2. recreation _____ _____ _____ _____

3. violation _____ _____ _____ _____

4. radiation _____ _____ _____ _____

5. appreciation _____ _____ _____ _____ _____

6. initiation _____ _____ _____ _____ _____

7. negotiation _____ _____ _____ _____ _____

8. association _____ _____ _____ _____ _____

Read these words in sentences.

1. The <u>creation</u> of a new <u>recreation</u> center will raise taxes.

2. High <u>radiation</u> from the power plant is a <u>violation</u> of the law.

3. I have no <u>appreciation</u> for this old book on cars.

4. The teachers' <u>association</u> started <u>negotiations</u> for a contract Thursday.

5. After the <u>initiation</u> service he will be a full member of the lodge.

Dictionary Marks and Less-Common Words

---

patient (pā′ shənt) **cautious** (kô′ shəs) **ancient** (ān′ shənt)

special (spesh′ əl) **spacious** (spā′ shəs) **partial** (pär′ shəl)

mission (mish′ ən) **mention** (men′ shən)

The syllables with *ti, ci,* and *si* that produce the *sh* sound are not accented.

1. Learning the Markings with Words You Know

Write the words after the respellings.

ancient   nation   partial   patient   pension   spacious

1. spā′ shəs _____   **4.** pär′ shəl _____

2. ān′ shənt _____   **5.** nā′ shən _____

3. pen′ shən _____   **6.** pā′ shənt _____

2. Writing More Difficult Words.
cia and *tia*

Write the words in the blanks.

confidential   mortician   optician   penitentiary

physician   potential   superficial   technician

1. It is _____ (kon′ fi den′ shəl) information that the new

   _____ (môr tish′ ən) may buy the land for a funeral

   home.

2. The X-ray _____ (tek nish′ ən) made only

   _____ (soo′ pər fish′ əl) remarks about the films, as if

   she understood little about my ailment.

138

3. Does your _____ (op tish´ ən) fit people for contact lenses?

4. The state needed a new _____ (pen´ ə ten´ shə rē) for the many drug offenders.

5. Our family _____ (fə zish´ ən) said the growth had the _____ (pə ten´ shəl) of becoming cancerous.

cious, tious, tien, cien

Write the words after the respellings.

| ambitious | contentious | ferocious |
| infectious | quotient | vicious |

1. in fekt´ shəs _____

2. fə rō´ shəs _____

3. vish´ əs _____

4. kən ten´ shəs _____

5. am bi´ shəs _____

6. kwō´ shənt _____

Read these words in sentences.

1. He was so <u>ambitious</u> to get ahead that he worked seven days a week.

2. The <u>quotient</u> is what you get when you divide one number by another.

3. The dog growled in a most <u>ferocious</u> way.

4. Chicken pox is a very <u>infectious</u> childhood disease.

5. Why is she so <u>contentious</u>? She argued about everything I said.

6. The paper printed a <u>vicious</u>, totally untrue story about the mayor.

tion, sion

Write the words in the blanks.

acceleration   automation   comprehension   conservation   depletion
frustration   ignition   persecution   pollination   precipitation

1. Robots, part of the _____ (ôt′ ə mā′ shən) program, replaced many workers in the plants.

2. He understood what he read; his _____ (kom′ prə hen′ shən) was excellent.

3. I felt the increased _____ (ək sel′ ə rā′ shən) of our car as we passed the truck.

4. The weather man forecasted light _____ (pri sip′ ə tā′ shən), but we got very heavy rain.

5. The serious _____ (di plē shən) of our own oil reserves forces us to import from other countries.

6. To reproduce, many plants depend on bee _____ (pol′ ə nā′ shən), the carrying of pollen from plant to plant.

7. He felt great _____ (frus trā′ shən) when he lacked the right parts for fixing his car.

8. In the desert the _____ (kon′ sər vā′ shən) of water is necessary.

9. Beatings and other forms of _____ (pur′ sə kyoo′ shən) are still carried on in some countries today.

10. The car wouldn't start because the _____ (ig ni′ shən) switch needed repairing.

140

3. Out-of-Pattern and Other Confusing Words

In a few but very useful words, the **sh** sound is produced by **sia, su, xu, xi, se,** and **ce**

Write the words after the respellings.

anxious	complexion	insurance	luxury	nauseous
ocean	pressure	Russian	sugar	tissue

1. ō′ shən _____

2. shoog′ ər _____

3. tish′ o͞o _____

4. luk′ shə rē _____

5. rush′ ən _____

6. presh′ ər _____

7. in shoor′ əns _____

8. nô shəs _____

9. aŋk′ shəs _____

10. kəm plek′ shən _____

Handling More *sh*-Sound Words . . . Lightly

Earning a Living

Circle what one can do to earn a living.

be a physician	work as an X-ray technician	show irritation
be a pediatrician	have a head-on collision	be a mortician
have a blood transfusion	be a musician with "The Temptations"	serve as a church missionary
be a politician	be a recreation supervisor	create air pollution
be a hair and nail specialist	be a park conservation officer	be a transmission specialist
sell insurance	be a mathematician	be a social worker
be a labor negotiator	watch "Confidential Agent"	be an auctioneer
live in a subdivision	sell residential property	fly to Russia for a vacation

Getting to Know You

Check the words that describe a person you would like to be around.

patient	gracious	ferocious	conscientious
compassionate	appreciative	antisocial	suspicious
ambitious	affectionate	artificial	nauseous
flirtatious	vicious	impatient	superstitious

Books for Children and Adults

Write *ch* after 9 titles children might enjoy reading or have read to them.

NBC Handbook
of Pronunciation

The Fire Station

Loudmouth Lucius

Your Financial
Planning Kit

Passion's Legacy

A Mouse Called
Junction

Confessions of a
Married Man

Devotions in the
Children's Hour

Intimate Connections

A Couple's Guide to
Communication

Overcoming Depression

Healing for Damaged
Emotions

The Subconscious
Mind

The Magician and Mr.
Tree

The Tiny Patient

Patricia and the
New Baby

I Can be an Electrician

Alicia and the Peacock

Helpful and Political Organizations

Write *1-1* (one to one) after 9 organizations that give direct help. Write *P* after 7 political groups that are trying to make broad changes.

Salvation Army

National Association for the
Advancement of Colored People

National Organization of Women

Coalition Against the Death Penalty

Post-Polio Connection

Relationships Anonymous

Committee for Conscientious Objection

Air Pollution Control Association

People for Environmental Protection

Compassionate Friends (for parents of
children who have died)

Childbirth Preparation Classes

Catholic Social Services

Congress for Racial Equality (CORE)

Post-Adoption Hotline

Project Transition (for mental patients)

Emotions Anonymous

TV Choices

Suppose you have only two TV Channels and no VCR. Which program would you choose? Circle your choice **or** cross out both programs if you turn off the set.

"Inside Edition" (news) OR **"The French Connection"** (movie)

"Imitation of Life" (movie) OR **"Cocaine: One Man's Seduction"** (documentary)

"Mortal Passions" (movie) OR **"National Geographic Special on Russia"**

"Assassination" (movie-drama) OR **"Operation Petticoat"** (TV comedy)

"Board of Education" (televised meeting) OR **"Mine Own Executioner"** (movie)

Concert: "Soul Vibrations" and **"Sweet Sensation"** OR **"Penitentiary"** (movie)

Chapter 12

The "Ghostly" Consonants and "Borrowed" Vowel Sounds

The Sound of **ch** as in
nature (nāʹ chər)

The Sound of **y** as in
million (milʹ yən)

The Sound of **k** as in
liquor (likʹ ər)

The Sound of Long **a** Spelled
by **e** as in **cafe´**(kə fāʹ), **ée** as in
fiancée (féʹ än sāʹ), and **et** as in
Chevrolet (shevʹ rə lāʹ)

The Sound of **w** as in
language (laŋʹ gwij)

The Sound of **zh** as in
vision (vizhʹ ən)

The Sound of Long **e** Spelled
by **i** as in **police** (pə lēsʹ)

The Sounded Final **e**
as in **recipe** (resʹ ə pē)

The "Ghostly" Consonants

You know about silent letters, which are *seen*, but not *heard*. In words with "ghostly consonants," letters are *heard*, but not *seen*. In some of the words there is a pattern, but for the others, you need to be aware of the existence of sounds that are not spelled by the usual letters. And you need to use the dictionary. (In the last chapter you dealt with the "ghostly" consonant sound of *sh*).

1. The Sound of *ch* as in **nature** (nā′ chər)

The sound of *ch* is produced by the spelling *tu* in many words.

Put *ch* over the part of the word that has the sound and then write the word in syllables.

1. statue   *stat*   *ue*

2. saturate   _____ _____ _____

3. century   _____ _____ _____

4. furniture   _____ _____ _____

5. adventure   _____ _____ _____

6. congratulate   _____ _____ _____ _____

7. moisture   _____ _____

8. spatula   _____ _____ _____

A few words that end in *tion* have the *ch* sound: **question** (kwes′ chən), **digestion** (di jes′ chən), **congestion** (kən jes′ chən), **combustion** (kəm bus′ chən). And so does **Christian** (kris′ chən).

Read some of these words with the *ch* sound in sentences.

1. I will congratulate him on his fine drawing of the Lincoln statue.

2. The house had furniture made in the last century.

3. The moisture from the spatula used to turn the hamburgers made the grease pop.

146

4. Fumes from <u>combustion</u> engines can cause <u>congestion</u> in the lungs.

5. On Sundays, traffic near <u>Christian</u> churches can be heavy.

6. She would <u>saturate</u> all the houseplants with water, and some died.

2. The Sound of *w* as in **language** (laŋ´ gwij)

Write the words after the respellings. Then, write *w* over the part of the word that makes the sound.

bilingual   distinguish   extinguish   genuine   penguin   persuade

1. jen´ yōō wən _gen̄uine_   4. pər swād´ _____

2. dis tiŋ´ gwish _____   5. peŋ´ gwin _____

3. bī liŋ´ gwəl _____   6. ik stiŋ´ gwish _____

Write the words in the lists. Then, write in *w* over the parts of the words that make the sound.

> Some of these words have both *ch* and *w* sounds.

actual   continual   factual   February   January   manual
mortuary   obituary   ritual   sanctuary   spiritual   statuary

ual	*uary*
actual	_____
_____	_____
_____	_____
_____	_____
_____	_____

Read some of these words with the _w_ sound in sentences.

1. The frightened refugees found <u>sanctuary</u> in churches and synagogues.

2. An <u>obituary</u> notice in the paper is a <u>factual</u> account of the dead.

3. The <u>mortuary</u> handles funerals but does not sell <u>statuary</u> for graves.

4. <u>Ritual</u> in churches is to promote a <u>spiritual</u> feeling in the congregation.

5. I tried to <u>persuade</u> the children to learn Spanish from their parents, so they would be <u>bilingual</u>.

6. She can't <u>distinguish</u> between a <u>genuine</u> diamond and a fake.

3. The Sound of the Consonant _y_ as in **Julia** (jōōl′ yə), **Daniel** (dan′ yəl), **million** (mil′ yən), **senior** (sēn′ yər), and **brilliant** (bril′ yənt)

The consonant sound of _y_ is heard in many _u_ words, as you learned in the _u_ chapter of _Book 1:_ **pure** (pyoor), **confuse** (kən fyooz′), **feud** (fyood), **Europe** (yoor′ əp). But the consonant _y_ sound is also heard in some words that don't have _u_.

_y_ə and _y_ə_l_

Write the words in the lists and put _y_ over the part of the word that makes the sound.

Australia   azalea   California   Cecilia   Daniel

magnolia   Nathaniel   Pennsylvania   petunia   Virginia   gardenia

| One word belongs in two lists. |

148

Names of People	Names of Places	Names of Plants
Cecila		
_____	_____	_____
_____	_____	_____
_____	_____	_____

yən, yər, yənt, yərd

Write the words that have the same vowel and consonant sound in the last syllable as the numbered words.

behavior	billiard	brilliant	bunion	champion
civilian	companion	communion	familiar	junior
lenient	onion	opinion	rebellion	savior

1. *yən* as in **union** (yoon′ yən) and **Italian** (i tal′ yən)

   _____ _____ _____ _____

   _____ _____ _____ _____

2. *yər* as in **senior** (sēn′ yər) and **peculiar** (pi kyool′ yər)

   _____ _____ _____ _____

3. *yənt* as in **convenient** (kən vēn′ yənt)

   _____ _____

4. *yərd* as in **Spaniard** (span′ yərd)

   _____

Read some of these words with the consonant *y* sound in sentences.

1. Cecelia planted azalea and gardenia bushes by the magnolia tree.

2. The billiard table was for both junior and senior army officers, but not for civilian personnel on the base.

3. I am familiar with the petunia, a flower of brilliant colors.

4. Daniel attended <u>union</u> meetings in <u>Pennsylvania</u> and <u>California</u>.

5. <u>Nathaniel</u> found the store <u>convenient</u>, but the clerk's <u>behavior</u> was often very <u>peculiar</u> toward him.

6. Many <u>Italians</u> settled in faraway <u>Australia</u>, in the South Pacific Ocean.

7. In Christian churches, the <u>Savior</u> is Jesus. Taking <u>communion</u> is part of the worship.

8. It is only my <u>opinion</u>, but I think the <u>champion</u> team might have won again if the coach hadn't been so <u>lenient</u> on training rules.

9. <u>Virginia</u> would be a better <u>companion</u> if she didn't talk about the <u>bunions</u> on her feet so often.

4. The Sound of **zh** as in **vision** (vizh′ ən), **Asia** (ā′ zhə), and **pleasure** (plezh′ ər)

Write the word that has the same vowel and consonant sound in the last syllable as the numbered word. Write zh over the part of the word that produces the sound.

casual   collision   division   explosion   exposure

leisure   measure   Persia   seizure   treasure   visual

1. pleasure   *expo(zh)sure*, _____, _____, _____, _____

2. usual   _____, _____

3. vision   _____, _____, _____

4. Asia   _____

> Three more words with the **zh** sound are: **Hoosier** (hoo′ zhər), **hosiery** (ho′ zhər e), and **magnesia** (mag ne′ zhə).

Read some of these words in sentences.

1. There was an <u>explosion</u> after the <u>collision</u> of two gas trucks.

2. He wore a <u>leisure</u> suit for <u>casual</u> events, such as class reunions.

3. We learned long <u>division</u> and how to <u>measure</u> a room for carpeting.

4. He had a <u>seizure</u> of coughing.

5. She drinks milk of <u>magnesia</u>, so chalky and thick, to improve digestion.

6. I had some <u>exposure</u> to <u>Hoosier</u> ways when I visited Indiana.

7. We <u>treasure</u> our <u>Persian</u> rug. It is a <u>visual</u> treat just to look at it.

5. The Sound of *k* as in **liquor** (lik′ ər)

The common sound of *qu* is *kw* as in **quick**. Some words from other languages have the *k* sound of *qu*. These words are not hard to read and spell once you know that *qu* in some words has the sound of *k*, and not *kw*.

Write the words in the blanks in which *k*, and not *kw*, is heard.

briquets	burlesque	conquer	croquettes	lacquer
masquerade	mosque	racquet	Roquefort	tourniquet

1. On Halloween we went to a _____ (mas′ kə rād′)
   dance.

2. The people of the Moslem faith worship in a
   _____ (mosk).

3. When her hand continued to bleed, they put a _____
   (toor′ nə kit) around the wrist.

4. The salmon _____ (krō kets′) have onions in them
   and are fried.

5. When using _____ (lak' ər), paint quickly before it dries.

6. Some strings on my tennis _____ (rak' it) broke.

7. We needed charcoal _____ (bri kets') to grill our steaks.

8. This white _____ (rōk' fərt) cheese dressing is for your salad.

9. He was a comic in a _____ (bər lesk') show.

10. Medical research cannot yet _____ (kon' kər) the head cold.

6. Spelling "Ghostly" Consonant Words with Common Endings

Write the words and add *ly*.

1. casual _____
2. usual _____
3. brilliant _____
4. natural _____

5. leisure _____
6. genuine _____
7. convenient _____
8. peculiar _____

Write the words and add *ing*, *ed*, and *er*.

1. treasure _____ _____ _____
2. question _____ _____ _____
3. extinguish _____ _____ _____

Write the words and add *es*.

1. century _____
2. mortuary _____
3. obituary _____

7. Prefixes/Beginnings and Suffixes/Endings

Write the related words in the blanks.

companionable   displeasure   familiar   indigestion   persuasive
punctuality   rebellious   reunion   unchristian

1. persuade   _____

2. Christian   _____

3. digest   _____

4. punctual   _____

5. union   _____

6. pleasure   _____

7. companion   _____

8. rebel   _____

9. family   _____

The "Borrowed" Vowels

The vowels of many words that have come into English, mainly from French, Spanish, and Italian, have remained unchanged. In some words, there is a pattern. For others, you need some experience in "handling" them, and you need the dictionary.

1. The Sound of Long *e* Spelled by *i* as in **gasoline** (gas′ ə lēn′), **police** (pə lēs′), and **antique** (an tēk′)

ine (ēn) as in **gasoline**

Write the 12 words that end with the long _e_ sound. Put a long _e_ over any _i_ that has that sound.

> Some words below don't have the long _e_ sound in the last syllable.

Christine	engine	limousine	machine	marine	Maxine
mezzanine	moonshine	nectarine	outline	Pauline	recline
routine	sardine	sunshine	tangerine	turpentine	vaccine
					valentine

Christ**ī**ne _____ _____

_____ _____ _____

_____ _____ _____

_____ _____ _____

ice (ēs) as in **police** and _ique_ (ēk) as in **antique**

Write the words in the syllables and put a long _e_ over the part of the word that makes the long _e_ sound.

1. antique   _an_   _t**ī**que_
2. police   _____ _____
3. Clarice   _____ _____
4. Maurice   _____ _____

5. physique   _____ _____
6. unique   _____ _____
7. technique   _____ _____
8. Bernice   _____ _____

Read some of these words in sentences.

1. Christine and Clarice made fruit salad of tangerines and nectarines.

2. Maurice has a good technique for repairing antique cars.

3. Lifting weights and staying with a routine of exercise helped him develop a great physique.

4. Bernice bought a sewing machine at the shop on the mezzanine floor that overlooks the lobby of the hotel.

154

5. Pauline thought a stretch <u>limousine</u> was <u>unique</u>, but actually there are many of them.

6. <u>Maxine</u> worked for the <u>police</u> department before joining the <u>Marines</u>.

More Words with the Long *e* Sound Spelled by *i*

Write the words after the respellings.

> Some "borrowed" words have *i* at the end, which has a long *e* (or short *i*) sound: **broccoli, spaghetti, chili, pepperoni, salami, Mimi**. There are more. Notice silent letters *s, ue, c.*

| bikini | debris | fatigue | liter | mosquito |
| paprika | petite | trio | visa | zucchini |

1. mə skēt′ ō _____
2. lēt′ ər _____
3. fə tēg′ _____
4. pə tēt′ _____
5. də brē′ _____

6. trē′ ō _____
7. pa prē′ kə _____
8. zo͞o kē′ nē _____
9. bi kē′ nē _____
10. vē′ zə _____

Read the words in sentences.

1. I suffer from <u>fatigue</u> because a <u>mosquito</u> kept me awake all night.

2. The fish on my plate was red with <u>paprika</u>, and the once-green <u>zucchini</u> looked dead.

3. You get more soda in a <u>liter</u> bottle than in the old quart.

4. She ate two servings of <u>spaghetti</u> and <u>chili</u>; how can she stay so <u>petite</u>?

5. Bernice hated the beach with all the half-naked, <u>bikini</u>-clad people and smelly <u>debris</u> scattered everywhere.

6. To enter some countries you must get special permission, a <u>visa</u>, from their government. Then you can use your <u>Visa</u> card there.

2. The Pronounced Final *e* as in **recipe**

The final *e* as in **recipe** (res′ ə pē) is pronounced in a few, but useful, words.

Write the 8 words in which the final *e* is pronounced.

Apache	apostrophe	blockade	catastrophe	furnace
karate	limestone	minestrone	pierce	posse
sesame	stampede	vigilante	volume	

_____ _____ _____

_____ _____ _____

_____ _____

Read these words in sentences.

1. <u>Apache</u> helicopters were named after an Indian tribe.

2. The movie showed a sheriff's <u>posse</u> riding off after a horse thief and a <u>vigilante</u> group forming to join the hunt.

3. We had <u>minestrone</u>, an Italian vegetable soup, and <u>sesame</u>-seed rolls.

4. One use of the <u>apostrophe</u>, a mid-air comma, is to show ownership.

5. The boy learned a mean kick in his <u>karate</u> class.

6. Which is a worse <u>catastrophe</u>, an earthquake or a big flood?

3. The Sound of Long $\bar{a}$ Spelled by *e* as in **café** (kə fā′), by *ee* as in **fiancée** (fē′ än sā′), and by *et* as in **Chevrolet** (shev′ rə lā′)

These syllables are at the end of the words.

> The accent mark is not always shown over the final *e* and *ee*.

Long $\bar{a}$ sound spelled by the final *e* and *ee*

Write the 8 words that have a final long *a* sound and put a long *a* over the part of the word that makes that sound.

> Don't forget to put in the accent mark (as seen below) that shows how to pronounce the final *e* and *ee*.

café	communicate	communiqué	consommé	consume
divorce	divorcée	fiancée	finance	rose
rosé	pure	purée	resumé	resume

> If you see **divorcé** and **fiancé**, with one *é*, it is a man.

café   _____   _____   _____

_____   _____   _____

Read some of these words with a long *a* sound spelled by *e* in sentences.

1. The dentist said I should <u>purée</u> all food until my gums healed.

2. France sent a <u>communiqué</u> to our government about a peace treaty.

3. He bought his <u>fiancée</u> a bottle of <u>rosé</u> wine.

4. The café made good chicken consommé, a clear soup.

5. There was no reason to include on her job resumé the fact that she was a divorcée.

> The long *a* sound spelled by *et* (as in **Chevrolet**) at the end of a word.

Write the 10 words that have the long *a* sound spelled by *et* and write long *a* over the part of the word that makes that sound.

| ballet | blanket | bouquet | buffet | bullet | cabaret | closet |
| croquet | crochet | filet | gourmet | ricochet | secret | valet |

$\overset{\bar{a}}{\textit{ball}\overset{}{\textit{e}}\textit{t}}$ _____ _____ _____ _____

_____ _____ _____ _____ _____

Read some of the words in sentences.

1. The ballet dancer received a big bouquet of roses.

2. Croquet is a lawn game played with wooden balls, metal hoops, and mallets.

3. The loud voices and music from the cabaret kept us awake all night.

4. A fish filet is supposed to be free of bones, but I usually find one.

5. Fine food is labeled gourmet, but now even hot dogs are called that.

6. He worked for the valet service of a hotel, pressing guests' clothing.

7. A bullet could ricochet off a building and kill someone.

8. The buffet supper was spread out on a long, elegant table.

Out-of-Pattern and Other Confusing Words

These are the "There-ought-to-be-a-law-against" words. They are common enough for you to notice.

☆ In a few words (from French) the long **o** sound is spelled by **eau**.

- **beau** (bō), a boyfriend or **beaux** (bō), several boyfriends
- **plateau** (pla tō′), high, level land
- **bureau** (byoor′ ō), a chest of drawers or a government agency
- **trousseau** (troo′ sō), a bride's outfit

You see place names (**Beaumont**) and family names (**Charbeneau**) with the long **o** sound spelled by **eau**. But two words, **beauty** (byoo′ tē) and **beautiful** (byoo′ tə fəl), have the long **u** sound.

☆ **choir** (kwīr), a group of people who sing together.

☆ **queue** (kyoo), a line you must wait in.

☆ **quay** (kē), a wharf of stone or concrete.

☆ **soldier** (sōl′ jər).

☆ **Philippines** (fil′ ə pēnz), the island counry, but **Filipino** (fil′ ə pē′ nō), the name of someone from the Philippines.

☆ **suit** (soot), a set of clothes, cards, etc. and **suite** (swēt), a group of connecting rooms or a set of matched furniture.

☆ **suede** (swād), rough-finished leather.

159

"How Do You Say and Spell Your Name?"

People with difficult names from other languages know they usually have to give help in pronunciation. Some of the phonics you learned in this chapter will help you with saying some names. In many languages, *i* has the long *e* sound. You know that **eau** or **eaux** has the long *o* sound. In some names, the unseen *y* is heard. You must try out names and apply what you know from saying similar names.

Try to pronounce the famous names using what you have learned in this chapter.

Boudreau	Thoreau	Houdini	Bedelia
Charisse	Jarreau	McDaniels	Beauregard
Champion	Mancini	Cochise	Cousteau
Borgnine	M. Ali	Santini	Valiant

Handling Words . . . Lightly

Rewards and Prizes

Circle what a company might offer as a reward for being a good worker.

A week at Padré Island National Seashore	A voyage to Juneau, AK	A tour of Eau Clair, WS library
A trip to the old city of St. Augustine, FL	Stretch limousine use for a day	Trip to the Statue of Liberty in NY harbor
A stay at Yosemite National Park	Tour of Magnolia Gardens, SC	Album "Grafitti Bridge" by Prince
Boat ride to Catalina Island, near Los Angeles	Gift certificate at Café Daphne	A picture by Prestige Photos of the boss
Trip to the Farm Bureau	Week at Wolverine Fitness Center	$50 at Unique Film and Video Store

Books: Keep or Pass On?

Circle the titles of books you might read once and then pass on to someone. The other books you might want to keep and refer to from time to time.

Rebellious Heart	The Corpse Had a Familiar Face
Women and Fatigue	The Marine Aquarium
An Inconvenient Woman	The Full Catastrophe Desk Reference
Black Stallion	Unnatural Causes
Masquerade	A Treasury of Baby Names
Union Forever	Winners' Guide to Casino Gambling
Conquering Shyness	Letters for All Occasions
Situation Tragedy	Casino Royale
The Frugal Gourmet Cookbook	Visions of the Heart

Automobile Words

Circle the 14 words you might read taking a class in automotive repair and working in a garage.

gasoline	Champion spark plugs	Chevrolet
machine tool	technique	billiards
temperature	combustion engine	Capri
spaniel	Festiva	genius
Buick Century	precision timing	corrosion
croquet	manual	Oldsmobile

Food-Service Words

Circle the 6 words you would probably not see in taking a food-service course and working in some restaurants and food stores.

sardines	measuring spoons	consommé	erosion
onions	buffet	filet	kiwi fruit
nectarines	penguins	zucchini	anesthesia
paprika	spatula	burlesque	tangerines
gourmet	minestrone soup	tortillas	rice pilaf
nicotine	croquettes	peas purée	café
recipes	sesame seeds	scallions	morphine

Post Office and Travel Words

Circle the 17 words you may need to read working in a post office, a mail shop, or a travel bureau.

Australia	Mobile, AL	Europe	Fritos
Philippines	Doritos	Tunisia	Beaumont, TX
Albuquerque, NM	Listerine	California	Vaseline
San Bernardino, CA	Rita's Burritos	Pennsylvania	Racine, WI
Virginia	Santa Fe, NM	Dominion of Canada	Saltines
Indonesia	Bordeaux, Fr.	Valvoline oil	Puerto Rico

Law-Enforcement Words

Circle the 15 words you might read in training for law-enforcement work.

police	behavior	ballet	routine
ricochet bullets	explosion	casualties	beauty shop
questioning	rebellions	trousseau	collision
vigilante	posse	valet	persuade
habitual criminal	catastrophe	civilian control	suede shoes

Famous Horses

Some horses are given some very peculiar names. <u>Circle the names of 12 famous horses.</u> The other names are of shops and other businesses.

Manuel	Genuine Risk	Career Resumés
Balloon Bouquets	Pasteurized	Look Sharp Valet Serv.
Unique Counters	Don Enrique	Classic Collision, Inc.
Polynesian	Foolish Pleasure	Mad Cupid Café
Jean Bereaud	Prestige Builders	Scottish Christian
Treasures & Antiques	Panique	Savior
Chateaugay	Comanche	Salty Dog Marina

And, now, if you want to go to a lake for a vacation, being a word handler, you can read the sign:

Lake Chargoggagaugmanchangagoggchanbunagungamaag, Maine— meaning, "You stay on your side of the lake, and I'll stay on mine."

© 1993 by REGENTS/PRENTICE HALL, A Division of Simon & Schuster, Englewood Cliffs, New Jersey 07632. All Rights Reserved.

Appendix

Selected Word List
from the
G.E.D. Practice Tests

The following lists of words were selected from the Official Practice Tests to be used before taking the General Educational Development tests (the G.E.D.). As you finish each chapter (and perhaps when you finish the book), look at the words to test yourself on decoding them. Some of the words you "handled" in the book, and some of them you did not. Of course, any word list deprives the reader of a very helpful aid in reading, seeing the word in the context of a sentence. And in preparing for the G.E.D., you will read about the ideas behind these words. But you have studied the elements of the words. Remember similar words you "handled" in the chapter, and remember the different ways words are built and the sounds letters make (and don't make). When you do this, the new words will come to you. If you should have any trouble with a word, go back and review the chapter in which this kind of word was dealt with. You will also benefit by looking up the word in the dictionary.

Chapter 1. *er, ir, ur*

1. affirm
2. appearances
3. bacteria
4. ceremonial
5. circuits
6. circumscribed
7. circumstances
8. emerged
9. emergencies
10. Europeans
11. generates
12. herbivore
13. Honduras
14. hurricanes
15. irrigating
16. materials
17. Nigeria
18. occurrences
19. premiered
20. researchers
21. stereo
22. suburban
23. superette
24. terminology
25. urban
26. urgency
27. urine

Chapter 2. *ar* and *or*

1. according
2. Antarctica
3. apparently
4. aristocracy
5. armada
6. armaments
7. caloric
8. capillary
9. carnivore
10. comparison
11. categories
12. creditworthiness
13. embarrassment
14. forager
15. forgery
16. forlorn
17. guarantee
18. guardians
19. historical
20. horizon
21. majority
22. marital
23. mortgages
24. opportunities
25. organism
26. paradise
27. parallel
28. parallelogram
29. paramedical
30. parasitic
31. summary
32. territory
33. unsanitary

Chapter 3. *oo*

1. balloon
2. bookkeeper
3. choosing
4. coos
5. flooding
6. footstool
7. Saskatoon
8. troop-carrying

Chapter 4. *oi, oy,* and *io*

1. avoided
2. biological
3. dandelions
4. destroyer
5. dioxide
6. disappointment
7. employer
8. enjoyment
9. oblivion
10. periodic
11. polio
12. scorpion
13. turmoil
14. unemployed
15. violated

Chapter 5. *au, aw*

1. astronauts
2. author
3. daughter
4. fraud
5. inaugural
6. laughter
7. mud-dauber
8. no-fault
9. sawdust

Chapter 6. *a* as in talk, *a* as in father

1. drama
2. quadrille
3. qualified
4. quantity
5. wasp

Chapter 7. *ou, ow*

1. accounting
2. allowed
3. boundaries
4. discourage
5. doubtful
6. droughts
7. encourage
8. enormous
9. flounder
10. gloriously
11. homogeneous
12. miscellaneous
13. numerous
14. obvious
15. previously
16. resources
17. seriously
18. spontaneous
19. surrounding
20. thoroughly
21. various

Chapter 8. *ie, ei*, and *ie*

1. achievement
2. audience
3. client
4. fortieth
5. eighteenth
6. experiences
7. foreign
8. Harriet
9. height
10. ingredients
11. Natalie
12. neighborhood
13. nutrients
14. proteins
15. relieved
16. scientific
17. scientists
18. society
19. species
20. unyielding
21. variety

Chapter 9. *y*

1. crystals
2. cyclorama
3. cylinder
4. cylindrical
5. Cynthia
6. hypothesis
7. hysteria
8. paralyze
9. Pythagorean
10. scythe
11. Sylvia
12. symbolize
13. Yvonne

Chapter 10. *ph, ch*

1. atmosphere
2. characteristics
3. chemical
4. choreographer
5. emphasize
6. geography
7. mechanism
8. melancholy
9. monarchy
10. orchestrator
11. orphanage
12. parachute
13. paragraph
14. photosynthesis
15. physical
16. psychologist
17. saprophytic
18. scholastic
19. sophisticated
20. technology
21. technological

Chapter 11. *sh* Spellings

1. administration
2. automation
3. commercial
4. Congressional
5. elimination
6. financial
7. foundation
8. generalization
9. glacier
10. gravitational
11. infectious
12. musician
13. negotiate
14. physician
15. professionalism
16. presidential
17. qualifications
18. reconstruction
19. stationary
20. sufficient
21. traditional
22. transaction
23. unconstitutional
24. voracious

Chapter 12. "Ghostly Consonants" and "Borrowed Vowels"

1. Australia
2. casualties
3. chlorine
4. combustion
5. composure
6. debris
7. erosion
8. extinguishing
9. eventually
10. familiarize
11. fiancé
12. intellectual
13. intrigued
14. measurements
15. mutualistic
16. oceanic
17. plateau
18. resumé
19. routinely
20. situations
21. undistinguishable
22. unique
23. usually
24. visualizing

Answer Key

To the teacher / tutor: More than one form of syllabication is given if the student has to write the syllables, since dictionaries often give one set of syllable breaks in the entry word and another one in the respelling. Flexibility is useful here as long as no more than one vowel sound is included in a syllable.

Chapter 1. *er, ir, ur*

Sound and Spelling

1. The Sound of *er* as in her, *ur* as in fur, and *ir* as in bird

Same Vowel Sound and Ending

1. (bur, her, spur, stir)
2. curd, herd, third
3. hurt, skirt, spurt
4. irk, jerk, Turk

Longer, Common Words with *er* as in **her**

1. (person)
2. modern
3. perfect
4. servant
5. thermos
6. sherbet
7. permit
8. sermon
9. lantern
10. verdict
11. alert
12. several

Longer, Common Words with *ur* as in **fur**

1. purchase
2. murder
3. nursery
4. current
5. burden
6. disturb
7. survive
8. sturdy
9. hurry
10. furnish
11. Saturday
12. surrender

Longer, Common Words with *ir* as in **bird**

1. thirty
2. birthday
3. dirty
4. Shirley
5. firsthand
6. squirrel
7. thirsty
8. girdle
9. confirm
10. Virgo
11. thirteen
12. skirmish

2. The Sound of *er* as in very

1. Jerry
2. sheriff
3. herring
4. merit
5. inherit
6. errand
7. Gerald
8. error
9. sterile

3. The Sound of Short *i* as in here, spirit, and pier

Write in *er*

1. here
2. mere
3. severe
4. sincere
5. hero

Write in *ir*

1. spirit
2. mirror

Write in *ier*

1. pier
2. pierce
3. fierce
4. cashier
5. frontier
6. brassiere

4. Spelling *ur*, *ir*, and *er* Words

Add *ing* and *ed*

1. (curling, curled)
2. jerking, jerked
3. confirming, confirmed
4. murdering, murdered
5. reserving, reserved
6. surprising, surprised

168

Add *s* or *es*

1. berries	5. flurries
2. hurries	6. girdles
3. curfews	7. nurseries
4. churches	8. curses

Syllables and Accents

1. Writing Words in Syllables

1. (mer′ chan dise)	7. ma ter′ ni ty
2. gov′ ern ment	8. cir′ cu lar
3. fu′ ner al	9. mir′ a cle
4. sur viv′ al *or*	10. cir′ cu late
sur vi′ val	11. ur′ gen cy
5. per′ ish a ble	12. al′ ler gy
6. ex per′ i ment	

2. *er* and *ir* Prefixes / Beginnings

1. per haps′	7. in ter vene′
2. su′ per vise	8. per′ se cute
3. per′ ma nent	9. cir cum′ fer ence
4. cir′ cum stan ces	10. su per son′ ic
5. in′ ter state	11. ir re sist′ i ble *or*
6. su per in tend′ ent	ir re sis′ ti ble
	12. ir res pon′ si ble

3. An *er* Suffix / Ending: *ery*

1. bak er y *or* ba ker y	5. shrub ber y
2. lot ter y	6. de liv er y
3. brib er y *or* bri ber y	7. re cov er y
4. gro cer y	8. up hol ster y

4. The Shifted Accent

1. (des′ ert, desert′)	4. convert′, con′ vert
2. permit′, per′ mit	5. in′ sert, insert′
3. per′ fect, perfect′	

5. Word Building

1. (per′ / son)
   per′′ / son / al
   per′′ / son / al / ly
   per′′ / son / al / ize
   per / son / al′′ / i / ty

2. ex / per′ / i / ment
   ex / per / i / men′ / tal
   ex / per / i / men′ / tal / ly

3. re / verse′
   re / vers′ / i / ble
   ir / re / vers′′ / i / ble *or* ir / re / ver′′ / si / ble

4. con / serve′
   con / serv′ / ing
   con / ser′′ / va / tive
   con / ser′′ / va / tive / ly

6. Split Vowels

iu

1. delirium
2. geranium
3. uranium

ia

1. (bacteria)	5. hernia
2. imperial	6. serial
3. cafeteria	7. material
4. perennial	8. intermediate

Dictionary Marks and Less-Common Words

1. Learning the Markings with Words You Know

1. (shirt)	6. nerve
2. berry	7. jerk
3. learn	8. furry
4. there	9. fury
5. miracle	10. sincere

2. Writing Less-Common Words

1. cherish, infirm	4. bursitis, dexterity
2. sterile, vermin	5. federal
3. heritage, reverence	6. mural

1. virile	6. turbulent
2. hibernate	7. generic
3. venereal	8. vertical
4. curriculum	9. terminate
5. conspiracy	10. affirmative

3. Silent Letters

1. (Pittsburgh)	5. answer
2. gherkin	6. rhinoceros
3. shepherd	7. cirrhosis
4. raspberry	5. Esther

Little Words in Longer Words

(Words to which only *s* or *es* could be added are not listed.)

1.

1. per, person, son, so, on, Al, lit, it
2. sup, super, per, up, in, ten, tend, den, dent, intend, end, superintend
3. per, ma, frost
4. con, on, cur, current, rent
5. the, he; her, mom, me, met, meter
6. imp, per, person, so, son, at, ate, on
7. in, firm, infirm, fir, it
8. as, asp, per, rat, rate, at, ate
9. term, in Al
10. term, in, at, ate, terminate

2.

1. in, ha, ham, am	5. bur, gun
2. Frank, ran, rank, fur	6. ran, rang, an, go
3. am, dam	7. germ, ma, man, many, any
4. church, chill, hill, ill	8. ham, am, bur, burg

Handling *er, ir,* and *ur* Words . . . Lightly

Informal Words

(Answers may vary.)

1. topsy-turvy	6. nerd
2. skullduggery	7. folderol
3. persnickety	8. hurly-burly
4. twerp	9. gurgle
5. nervy	10. jerk

Places or Brands?

(Answers may vary.)

New Jersey, Poverty Hill, Perseverance, Pittsburgh, Deliverance, Merrymeeting, Skunk's Misery, Germany, Burden, Liberia, Burnt Ranch, Vermont, Prosperity, Virgin, Siberia

Medical Words

mermaid, tabernacle, currency, merchandise, federal, earthquake, Terence

Paid for by Our Tax Dollars?

Kentucky Derby race track, Burlington Industries, Pillsbury Mills, Sheraton Hotels, Fertilizer plants, Xerox Company, Murder Burger, Pittsburgh Pirates

What's New?

1, 3, 5, 6, 7, 10, 11, 12, 13

Choosing a Product Name

(Answers may vary.)

Bolero, Surrender, Emerald, Vera, Dark Amber, On the Terrace

Chapter 2.   *ar* and *or*

Sound and Spelling

1. The Sounds of *ar* as in **car**, **carry**, and **war**.

Same Vowel Sound and Ending: *ar* as in **car**

1. card, lard, yard
2. bark, mark, spark
3. harp

Longer, Common Words with *ar*

1. carton	9. parent
2. narrow	10. garlic
3. harvest	11. parrot
4. quarrel	12. wardrobe
5. barbecue	13. welfare
6. radar	14. barren
7. bargain	15. artery
8. warrant	16. garment

2. The Sounds of *or* as in **corn** and in **word**

Same Vowel Sound and Ending: *or* as in **corn**

1. born, thorn, torn
2. dorm, storm
3. cork, pork, stork

Longer, Common Words with *or*

1. forest	7. moral
2. porter	8. resort
3. worthy	9. workshop
4. hornet	10. worthwhile
5. worship	11. florist
6. tornado	12. worldwide

3. Spelling *ar* and *or* Words

Add *er*

1. carrier	**4.** stormier
2. darker	**5.** scarier
3. worthier	**6.** former

Add *s* or *es*

1. worries	**5.** garters
2. marches	**6.** marbles
3. stars	**7.** marries
4. stories	**8.** porches

Add *age*

1. marriage	**2.** carriage

Syllables and Accents

1. Writing Words in Syllables

1. im por′ tant	**7.** em bar′ rass
2. marsh′ mal low	**8.** war′ ran ty
3. sup port′ ive	**9.** trans par′ ent
4. ar′ gu ment	**10.** cor re spond′
5. wors′ en ing	**11.** par tic′ i pate
6. hor′ ri ble	**12.** char′ i ta ble

2. *ar* and *or* Suffixes / Endings

ary as in **voluntary**; *ory* as in **directory**

ary: anniver′sary, sec′retary, cus′tomary, li′brary, nec′cessary
ory: acces′sory, introduc′tory, lav′atory, satisfac′tory, ter′ritory

3. Word Building

1. or′ / der	**3.** ar′ / gue
or′ / der / ly	ar′ / gu / ing
dis / or′ / der	ar′ / gu / ment
dis / or′ / der / ly	ar / gu / men′ / ta / tive
dis / or′ / der / li / ness	
2. part	**4.** nor′ / mal
par / tic′ / i / pate	nor′ / mal / ly
par / tic′ / i / pant	ab / nor′ / mal
par / tic′ / i / pa / ting	nor′ / mal / ize
	ab / nor / mal′ / i / ty

4. Split Vowels

ia

(his / to / ri / an *or* his / tor / i / an)
jan / i / to / ri / al *or* jan / i / tor / i / al
li / brar / i / an
ma / lar / i / a
me / mo / ri / al *or* me / mor / i / al
sen / a / to / ri / al *or* sen / a / tor / i / al
var / i / ance
veg / e / tar / i / an

Write Words in the Blanks:

1. librarian	**5.** malaria
2. vegetarian	**6.** historian
3. memorial	**7.** senatorial
4. janitorial	**8.** variance

iu, ea, eo

1. aquarium	**5.** Korea
2. planetarium	**6.** deodorant
3. crematorium	**7.** area
4. sanitarium	

Dictionary Marks and Less-Common Words

1. Learning the Markings with Words You Know

1. bar	**5.** worst
2. born	**6.** doctor
3. ward	**7.** beggar
4. square	**8.** blare

2. Writing Less-Common Words

1. porcelain	**5.** carcinogen
2. garnishee	**6.** arbitrator
3. parallel	**7.** horizon
4. carnage	**8.** torrent

1. cardiogram	**6.** paralegal
2. commissary	**7.** cartilage
3. dormant	**8.** marinade
4. parliament	**9.** Arabic
5. ordinance	**10.** mortality

3. Silent Letters

Silent *h*, *g*, *u*

Silent *h*: Deborah, honor, rhubarb, sorghum
Silent *g*: arraign
Silent *u*: guarantee, guardian, guitar, morgue

Other Silent-Letter Words

1. jeøpardy
2. parfait̸ or parfai̸t
3. corp̸s̸
4. sẃord
5. ćzar, t̸sar
6. mor̸tgagé or mor̸tgage
7. p̸soriasis
8. corpusćlé or corpusćle

Little Words in Longer Words

1.

1. harm, arm, on
2. par, part, art, is, an
3. art, till, tiller, ill
4. art, choke, tic
5. for, form, or, late, at, ate
6. par, son, pa, parson, so, age, on, arson, nag
7. is, me, mean, an, or demeanor
8. art, tic, late, at, ate
9. as, par, asp, Gus, rag, us
10. imp, import, port, or, tan, an

2.

1. car, carbon, on, dale, Al, ale
2. nor, Norm, Norman, an, or, man, and, Andy
3. ma, am, mama, mar, on, neck, Ron
4. mad, ad, gas, scar, Ada, car
5. law, war, ware, are
6. or, land, do, and
7. for, form, or
8. an, ant, arc, tar, tic, Arctic
9. Lea, leaven, leave, worth, wort, or

Handling *ar* and *or* Words . . . Lightly

Suitable Words

(Answers may vary.)

smarty-pants, worry-wart, malarkey, ignorant, subnormal, dorky, varmint, blarney, moron, stubborn, lardhead, garbage

Jobs: Indoor or Outdoor?

Ozarks forest ranger, Antarctic explorer, collecting garbage and refuse, marble quarry foreman, catching sharks for the aquarium

A Little Too Clever?

(Answers may vary.)

Marvel, Pillar to Post, The Orange Crate, Great Performances, Old Horizons

Magazines

Car and Driver
Harper's
Inside Sports
Motor Trends
Parents
New York Magazine
Sports Illustrated
Organic Gardening
Forum
Vegetarian Times
Parenting

Names and Nicknames

(Answers may vary.)

Hell's Forty Acres
Land of Opportunity
Port of Missing Men
Hornet's Nest
Land of Lizard
Heart of Dixie
Tarheel
Porkopolis
Garden
Corncracker
Cornopolis
Peace Garden
Cornhusker
Buzzard
Lone Star

Gifts

(Answers will vary.)

Chapter 3.   *oo*

Sound and Spelling

1. The Sound of *oo* as in **moon**

Same Vowel Sound and Ending

1. brood, mood
2. stoop, swoop, troop
3. loot, toot
4. goose, moose, noose
5. boom, broom

Longer, Common Words with *oo* as in **moon**

1. shamp*oo*
2. r*oo*ster
3. mushr*oo*m
4. t*oo*thpaste
5. racc*oo*n
6. n*oo*dle
7. p*oo*dle
8. sc*oo*ter
9. h*oo*ray
10. f*oo*lpr*oo*f
11. teasp*oo*n
12. whirlp*oo*l
13. whiskbr*oo*m
14. t*oo*lbox
15. rustpr*oo*f
16. l*oo*phole

2. The Sound of *oo* as in **book**

Same Vowel Sound and Ending

1. stood, wood
2. brook, cook, crook, hook, shook, took

Longer, Common Words with *oo* as in **book**

1. hardw**oo**d	7. b**oo**kkeeper
2. c**oo**kie	8. underst**oo**d
3. f**oo**thold	9. w**oo**dchuck
4. handb**oo**k	10. baref**oo**t
5. fishh**oo**k	11. c**oo**kb**oo**k
6. motherh**oo**d	12. g**oo**dl**oo**king

3. Spelling *oo* Words

Add *ing*, *ed*, and *er*

1. cooking, cooked, cooker
2. rooming, roomed, roomer
3. looting, looted, looter
4. shampooing, shampooed, shampooer

Add *er*, *est*

1. moodier, moodiest	4. spookier, spookiest
2. gloomier, gloomiest	5. bloodier, bloodiest
3. roomier, roomiest	

Syllables and Accents

1. Writing Words in Syllables

1. hon′ ey moon	5. loos′ en ing
2. cook′ er y	6. fool′ ish ness
3. broth′ er hood	7. fool′ hard y *or* fool′ har dy
4. crook′ ed ness	8. sooth′ ing ly

Dictionary Marks and Less-Common Words

1. Writing Less-Common Words

1. caboose	6. taboo
2. lagoon	7. cocoon
3. platoon	8. cartoon
4. festoon	9. boomerang
5. macaroon	10. hoodwink

Little Words in Longer Words

1. ran, rang, an, go, goo, goon, on	6. bloom, blooming, loom, looming, in, on, ton
2. Al, lam, am, ma, zoo	7. chat, at, hat, ah, hooch
3. liver, live, pool	8. bloom, loom, bur, burg
4. brook, rook, have, haven	9. mat, at, to, too
5. woo, on, sock, socket	

Handling Words . . . Lightly

Addresses or Movie Titles

Kalamazoo, MI	Wooster, OH
Baraboo, WI	Tuscaloosa, AL
Chattanooga, TN	Woonsocket, RI
Yazoo City, MS	Goodnight, TX
Oskaloosa, IA	

Name the Business

(Answers will vary.)

Animals?

raccoon, rooster, cuckoo, kangaroo, cockatoo, moose, poodle, baboon, rook, woodchuck, mongoose, loon

Chapter 4.   *oi, oy* and *io*

Sound and Spelling

1. The Sound of *oi* as in **oil** and *oy* as in **boy**

Same Vowel Sound and Ending

1. hoist	4. Lloyd
2. joint	5. foil
3. Roy, toy	6. Joyce, voice

Longer, Common Words with *oi*

1. tinf**oi**l	7. g**oi**ter
2. t**oi**let	8. rec**oi**l
3. p**oi**son	9. av**oi**d
4. inv**oi**ce	10. rej**oi**ce
5. app**oi**nt	11. temderl**oi**n
6. sirl**oi**n	12. n**oi**sy

Longer, Common Words with *oy*

1. ann**oy**	7. **oy**ster
2. destr**oy**	8. s**oy**bean
3. empl**oy**	9. v**oy**age
4. enj**oy**	10. ah**oy**
5. l**oy**al	11. b**oy**hood
6. r**oy**al	12. b**oy**cott

2. Spelling *oi* and *oy* Words

Add *ing*, *ed*, and *er*

1. boiling, boiled, boiler
2. pointing, pointed, pointer
3. destroying, destroyed, destroyer

173

Syllables and Accents

1. Writing Words in Syllables

1. loy′ al ly
2. oint′ ment
3. en joy′ a ble
4. un en joy′ a ble
5. cor′ du roy
6. noise′ less ly
7. dis ap point′ ment
8. em broi′ der y

2. Word Building

1. em / ploy′
   em / ploy / ee′ *or*
   em / ploy′′ / ee
   em / ploy′′ / er
   em / ploy′′ / ment
   em / ploy′′ / a / ble

2. an / noy′
   an / noy′′ / ing
   an / noy′′ / ance

3. a / void′
   a / void′′ / ance
   a / void′′ / a / ble
   un / a / void′′ / a / ble

3. Split-Vowel Words

io-Put a slash between the syllables

(an / ti / bi / ot / ic)
li / on
O / hi / o
pi / o / neers
vi / o / late
id / i / ot
Li / o / nel
pa / ti / o
ra / di / o
vi / o / lin

Write Words in the Blanks

1. Lionel, radio
2. idiot, lion
3. antibiotic
4. pioneers, Ohio
5. violin
6. patio
7. violate

Write Syllables as Whole Words

1. tapio′ca
2. vi′olet
3. biol′ogy
4. di′ocese
5. i′odine
6. bi′opsy

Dictionary Marks and Less-Common Words

1. Writing Less-Common Words

1. steroid
2. mastoid
3. convoy
4. exploit
5. loiter
6. deploy
7. turquoise
8. alloy
9. asteroid
10. Mongoloid

2. Silent Letters

1. moisten
2. rheumatoid
3. buoyant
4. hemorrhoids

Little Words in Longer Words

1. hot, point, in
2. she, he, boy, an
3. live, liver, no, is
4. to, toy
5. ill, in, no, is
6. boy, kin, in
7. per, am, boy
8. trap, ape, rap, rape

Handling *oi* and *oy* Words . . . Lightly

Medical Words

coins, tinfoil, embroider, bellboy, patriot, spoilsport, broiler

Businesses Names

(Answers may vary.)

The Sirloin Strip
Curiousity Shop
The Hare and Tortoise
   Running Shop
Killroy Bar & Grill
Tif-Toi Poodle Groomers
The Pet Spoilers
Canine Clip Joint

Words, Good and Bad

(Answers will vary.)

g loyal
b unemployed
g rejoice
b annoying
b poisoned
b loitering
b violated
g heroic
b idiotic
b exploited
b noisy
b turmoil
b disappointed
g joyful
b spoiled
b rheumatoid
g noiseless
b destroyed

Road Signs

Ferry to Isle Royale
Hotpoint Service Center
Leaving Doyelston—
   Come Back Soon
Crown Point City Limits
Oyster Bay Welcomes
   You
Re-elect Senator
   Moynihan
Ohio Turnpike Next Left
Visit Historic Croyden

Chapter 5.   *au* and *aw*

Sound and Spelling

1. The Sound of *au* as in **Paul** and *aw* as in **saw**

Same Vowel Sound and Ending

1. dawn, drawn, fawn, pawn
2. flaw, slaw, straw, thaw
3. brawl, crawl, haul
4. vault

Longer, Common Words with *au*

1. l*au*ndry	9. exh*au*st
2. f*au*lty	10. *au*to
3. s*au*sage	11. f*au*cet
4. s*au*na	12. bec*au*se
5. l*au*nder	13. *au*thor
6. d*au*ghter	14. appl*au*se
7. s*au*cer	15. apples*au*ce
8. *Au*gust	16. *au*tumn

Longer, Common Words with *aw*

1. dr*aw*er	5. *aw*ning
2. l*aw*yer	6. fl*aw*less
3. *aw*kward	7. jigs*aw*
4. *aw*ful	8. withdr*aw*n

2. Spelling *au* and *aw* Words

Add *ing*, *ed*, and *er*

1. hauling, hauled, hauler
2. brawling, brawled, brawler
3. laundering, laundered, launderer
4. exhausting, exhausted

Syllables and Accents

1. Writing Words in Syllables

1. res′ tau rant	7. au′ di tor
2. o ver haul′	8. awk′ ward ly
3. man′ slaugh ter	9. un law′ ful
4. som′ er sault	10. aw′ ful ly
5. Laun′ dro mat	11. straw′ ber ry
6. au′ top sy	12. naugh′ ti ness

2. Word Building

1. au′ / to
   au′ / to / mate
   au / to / mat′ / ic
   au / to / mo′ / tive

2. au′ / thor
   au′ / thor / ship
   au′ / thor / ize
   au / thor′ / i / ty
   au / thor′ / i / ta / tive

3. au′ / dit
   au′ / di / tor
   au′ / di / ble
   au′ / di / tor / y

4. ex / haust′
   ex / haust′ / ed
   ex / haus′ / tive
   ex / haust′ / i / ble

3. Split-Vowel Words

1. au di o	4. mau so le um
2. Clau di a	5. au di tor i um
3. Aus tri a	6. au thor i tar i an

Dictionary Marks and Less-Common Words

1. Learning the Markings with Words You Know

1. pawn	4. draw
2. fault	5. haul
3. slaw	6. law

2. Writing Less-Common Words

1. gaudy	7. caustic
2. authentic	8. plausible
3. default	9. brawny
4. auburn	10. inaugurate
5. jaundice	11. awesome
6. Holocaust	12. thesaurus

Little Words in Longer Words

1. ha, haw, hawk, kin, in, aw
2. crawl, craw, raw, awl, aw
3. claw, law, aw, so, son, on
4. ha, haw, thorn, or, horn, aw
5. sag, in, gin, aw
6. was, wash, as, ash, ten, aw
7. raw, so, son, on, ill, aw
8. war, saw, aw
9. saw, aw
10. laud, hi, hill, ill
11. law, ton, on, aw, to
12. at, tuck

Handling *au* and *aw* Words . . . Lightly

Place Names

(Answers may vary.)

Milwaukee	Dinosaur	Chautauqua
Maumee	Shawnee	Waukegan
Wausau	Escatawpa	Kennesaw
Pawnee	Mohawk	Paw Paw
Wauwatosa	Choctaw	Gnaw Bone
Massauga	Austria	Secaucus
Sawhill	Slaughter	

Headlines

1, 3, 4, 6, 8, 10, 11

Judgment Words

(Answers may vary.)

naughty boy
plausible reason
authoritarian father
awkward dancer
dawdling worker
withdrawn child

awesome thunderstorm
assault and battery
fraudulent deal
scrawny woman
awful job
faulty product

Classic Movies

The Pawnbroker
The Prince and the
  Pauper
Slaughterhouse 5
The Awful Truth

Lawrence of Arabia
Little Lord Fauntleroy
Drums Along the
  Mohawk
The Outlaw

Science Words

lawyers
Santa Claus
laundry
applesauce

sausage
somersaults
heehaw
Austin, TX

Chapter 6. Two More Sounds of *a*

Sound and Spelling

1. The Sound of *a* as in **talk**

Same Vowel Sound and Ending

1. balk, chalk, stalk, walk
2. ball, fall, mall, stall
3. malt, salt, Walt
4. scald

Longer, Common Words with *a* as in **talk**

1. w*a*lnut
2. *a*lso
3. *a*lmost
4. f*a*lse
5. w*a*ltz
6. *a*lways
7. sm*a*llpox
8. inst*a*ll
9. *a*llspice
10. h*a*lter
11. h*a*llway
12. f*a*lsely
13. f*a*llen
14. *a*lter
15. *a*ltar

2. The Sound of *a* as in **father**

palm, squad, what, squash, squat, swatch, calm, swat

Longer, Common Words with *a* as in **father**

1. m*a*ma
2. p*a*pa
3. sw*a*llow
4. cors*a*ge
5. mass*a*ge
6. gar*a*ge
7. qu*a*ntity
8. qu*a*lity

3. Spelling *a* as in **father**, and as in **talk**

Add *ing*, *ed*, and *er*

1. walking, walked, walker
2. squatting, squatted, squatter
3. calming, calmed, calmer
4. wadding, wadded
5. watching, watched, watcher

Syllables and Accents

1. Writing Words in Syllables

1. wall′ pa per
2. salt′ shak er *or*
   salt′ sha ker
3. talk′ a tive
4. watch′ ful ness
5. fa′ ther hood
6. salt′ i ness
7. in stall′ ment
8. gall′ blad der
9. wash′ a ble
10. qual′ i ty
11. quan′ ti ty
12. pall′ bear er

Dictionary Marks and Less-Common Words

1. Learning the Markings with Words You Know

1. bald
2. scald
3. what
4. watt
5. wad
6. all
7. swatch
8. calm
9. salt
10. mall
11. squat
12. squash

2. Writing Less-Common Words

1. Baltic
2. balsa
3. falter
4. appalled
5. cobalt
6. Balkans
7. alderman
8. almanac

1. lava
2. lager
3. embalm
4. squalor
5. Islam
6. squadron
7. Talmud
8. swastika
9. Slavic
10. squabble

Handling More *a* Words . . . Lightly

Books into Movies

(Answers may vary.)

The Godfather	The Tightwad
The Great Waltz	Life with Father
Rose of Panama	The Squall
Two Wanderers	The Swan
The Saint of Palm Springs	A Fish Called Wanda
The Alderman	Moonlight on the Wabash
Night Stalker	Death at Lake Tahoe
Quality Street	

Street Names

(Answers may vary.)

Looking for a Job

(Answers may vary.)

Dalton Books	Food Squad
Quality Pest Control	Yamaha Motorsports
Chimney Rescue Squad	Auto Plaza
An Ultimate Massage	Suwanee Leather Co.
Aqua World	Walgreen's Drug Store
Ramada Inn	

Having a Holiday

(Answers may vary.)

Lava Hot Springs, CA	Lake Tahoe, NV
Walnut Canyon, AZ	Baldwin Lake, MI
Okefenokee Swamp, GA	Walden Pond, MA
Minnehaha Falls, MN	

Chapter 7. *ou* and *ow*

Sound and Spelling

1. The Sound of *ou* as in out, and *ow* as in how

Same Vowel Sound and Ending

1. bound, hound, pound
2. blouse, mouse
3. couch, crouch, grouch
4. scour, sour
5. clown, drown, frown, town
6. fowl, owl, prowl

Longer, Common Words *ou* Words

1.	around	7.	mountain
2.	aloud	8.	announce
3.	amount	9.	discount
4.	trousers	10.	county
5.	surround	11.	pronounce
6.	fountain	12.	thousand

Longer, Common *ow* Words

1.	flower	5.	coward
2.	power	6.	allow
3.	towel	7.	chowder
4.	vowel	8.	township

2. Other Sounds of *ou*

Same Vowel Sound and Ending

1. brought, fought, ought, thought
2. soup
3. should, would
4. rough, tough
5. though

Longer, Common Words with Other *ou* Sounds

1.	southern	11.	shoulder
2.	tourist	12.	although
3.	cousin	13.	double
4.	youngster	14.	souvenir
5.	country	15.	boulder
6.	trouble	16.	detour
7.	couple	17.	Louis
8.	coupon	18.	furlough
9.	boulevard	19.	Douglas
10.	thorough	20.	cantaloupe

3. Spelling *ou* and *ow* Words

Add *ing*, and *ed*

1.	souring, soured	3.	grouping, grouped
2.	howling, howled	4.	detouring, detoured

Add *s* or *es*

1. counties
2. countries
3. pounds
4. houses
5. couches
6. pronounces

Syllables and Accents

1. Writing Words in Syllables

1. youth' ful
2. pow' er ful
3. an nounce' ment
4. mis pro nounce'
5. trou' ble some
6. doubt' less
7. nour' ish ment
8. sour' ness
9. cow' ard ly
10. en cour' age ment
11. thought' ful ness
12. tour' na ment

2. An *ou* Prefix / Beginning, *counter*

1. coun ter act
2. coun ter sign
3. coun ter bal ance
4. coun ter clock wise

3. An *ou* Suffix / Ending, *ous*

1. fa'mous
2. nerv'ous *or* ner'vous
3. haz'ardous
4. poi'sonous
5. coura'geous
6. dan'gerous
7. can'cerous
8. nu'merous
9. moun'tainous
10. hu'morous

4. Split Vowels in *ous* Words

1. se ri ous *or* ser i ous
2. stren u ous
3. te di ous
4. cour te ous
5. con spic u ous
6. con tin u ous
7. de lir i ous
8. mis cel la ne ous

5. *ous* Words and the Shifted Accent

1. en'vious
2. glo'rious *or* glor'ious
3. victo'rious *or* victor'ious
4. var'ious
5. inju'rious *or* injur'ious
6. indus'trious

Dictionary Marks and Less-Common Words

1. Learning Markings with Words You Know

1. house
2. drown
3. thought
4. would
5. howl
6. soup
7. though
8. rough
9 dough
10. mouse
11. sour
12. tough

2. Writing Less-Common Words

ou as in **out** and *ow* as in **how**

1. gouge
2. allowance
3. devour
4. bounty
5. Bowery
6. pronoun
7. impound
8. devout
9. astound
10. endowment

The Other *ou* Sounds

1. nougat
2. poultry
3. coupling
4. bourbon
5. vermouth
6. croutons
7. velour
8. wrought

More Words with Other *ou* Sounds

1. borough
2. trough
3. mourns
4. louver
5. contour
6. goulash
7. acoustical
8. poultice

Handling *ou* and *ow* Words . . . Lightly

Places to Visit

(Answers will vary.)

Book Titles

The Hill of Evil Counsel
The Fountainhead
Journey to the Center of the Earth
Dirty Rotten Scoundrels
Rough and Tender
Uncommon Vows

The Benefit of the Doubt
Boundaries
Mutiny on the Bounty
New Orleans Mourning
The Perfect Furlough
Shroud for a Nightingale

What's a Good Employee?

(Answers may vary.)

serious, industrious, curious, courteous, thorough, courageous, sound, resourceful, thoughtful, well-nourished

Telephone Book Listings

The Cat's Meow
Doubleday Book Shop
Thoroughbred Lounge
Sourdough Baker
Astounding Clowning
Fabulous Food
Discount Batteries
Pigs' Trough Lounge

Chapter 8. *ie*, *ei*, and *ie*

Sound and Spelling

1. The Long *e* Sound of *ie* in **yield** and *ei* in **neither**

Same Vowel Sound and Ending

1. field, shield, wield
2. piece
3. brief, chief, grief
4. grieves

Longer, Common *ie* Words with the Long *e* Sound

1. rel*ie*f
2. rel*ie*ve
3. mov*ie*
4. bel*ie*f
5. bel*ie*ve
6. ach*ie*ve
7. d*ie*sel
8. ap*ie*ce
9. brown*ie*
10. coll*ie*
11. br*ie*fcase
12. Mar*ie*

Longer, Common *ei* Words with the Long *e* Sound

1. c*ei*ling
2. *ei*ther
3. rec*ei*pt
4. caff*ei*ne
5. conc*ei*ted
6. rec*ei*ve
7. Sh*ei*la
8. dec*ei*ve

2. The Sound of *ei* as in **eight**

1. freight, weight
2. rein, reign
3. sleigh

3. Spelling *ie*, and *ei* Words

Add *ing*, *ed*, and *s*

1. weighing, weighed, weighs
2. yielding, yielded, yields
3. grieving, grieved, grieves
4. piecing, pieced, pieces

Add *er*, *ed*, and *s*

1. believing, believed, believes
2. deceiving, deceived, deceives
3. receiving, received, receives

Syllables and Accents

1. Writing Words in Syllables

1. bat′ tle field
2. cal′ o rie
3. neigh′ bor ly
4. ra′ bies
5. de ceit′ ful
6. un veiled′
7. dis be lief′
8. a chieve′ ment
9. griev′ ance *or* grie′ vance
10. un weighed′

2. Split-Vowels in *ie* Words

1. di′ et
2. qui′ et
3. cli′ ent
4. pli′ ers
5. sci′ ence
6. fi′ er y
7. So′ vi et
8. a′ li en
9. Vi et nam′
10. Vi en′ na

1. variety
2. society
3. anxiety
4. orient
5. oriental
6. experience
7. obedience
8. ingredient
9. recipient
10. audience

Dictionary Marks and Less-Common Words

1. Learning the Markings with Words You Know

1. vein
2. shield
3. sleigh
4. Neil
5. weight
6. piece
7. seize
8. brief
9. Keith
10. freight

2. Writing Less-Common Words

1. codeine
2. reprieve
3. conceive
4. aggrieved
5. protein
6. surveillance
7. perceive
8. besieged

3. Out-of-Pattern, Confusing Words

1. sieve
2. heirloom
3. heist
4. heifer
5. Geiger
6. feisty
7. foreign
8. Fahrenheit, forefeit
9. counterfeit, mischief
10. sleight

Handling *ie* and *ei* Words . . . Lightly

The Business Pages of the Phone Book

Den of Thieves
Oriental Foods and Supply
Old Heidelberg Inn
Detroit Diesel, Inc.
Consolidated Freight Ways
A-Plus Dog Obedience School
Eightball Saloon
H.J. Heinz Company
The Heights and the Pits

Movie Titles?

Fiendish Caffeine, Surveillance of the Weight
Watchers, Neighborly Achievement, Protein Place,
Falling Ceilings, Diesel Engines, Neither, Battlefield
Heebie-Jeebies

Chapter 9.   The Vowel *y*

Sound and Spelling

1. The Sound of *y* in **cry** and **gym**

The Long *i* Sound of *y*

by, cry, dry, Hy, Lyle, ply, pry, rhyme, shy, sky, sly,
spry, style, try, type

The Short *i* Sound of *y* as in **gym**

1. (gym)
2. hymn
3. rhythm
4. Lynn
5. lynx
6. gyp
7. cyst
8. lynch
9. crypt
10. myth

Longer, Common *y* Words

1. nylon
2. syrupy
3. hygiene
4. symptom
5. cyclist
6. Sydney
7. plywood
8. satisfy
9. typist
10. crystal
11. system
12. bicycle

2. Spelling *y* Words

Add *ing*, *ed*, and *es*

1. crying, cried, cries
2. trying, tried, tries
3. applying, applied, applies
4. relying, relied, relies

Add *ance*

1. reliance
2. defiance
3. alliance
4. appliance

Syllables and Accents

1. Writing Words in Syllables

1. dy' na mite
2. par' a lyze
3. sym' pa thy
4. mys' ter y
5. Car' o lyn
6. cyl' in der
7. re cy' cle
8. cy' clist
9. gym nas' tics
10. am' e thyst
11. Mar' i lyn
12. hy po der' mic

2. The Shifted Accent

1. (sys tem at' ic *or*
   sys te mat' ic)
2. dy nam' ic
3. ap' pli cant
4. symp to mat' ic
5. pa ral' y sis
6. spe cif' ic

3. Word Building

1. sym'' / pa / thy
   sym'' / pa / thize
   sym / pa / thet' / ic
   sym / pa / thet' / i / cal / ly
2. mys'' / ter / y
   mys / te' / ri / ous *or* mys / ter' / i / ous
   mys / te' / ri / ous / ly *or* mys / ter' / i / ous / ly
   mys / te' / ri / ous / ness *or*
   mys / ter' / i / ous / ness
3. an'' / a / lyze
   an'' / a / lyst
   a / nal' / y / sis
   an / a / lyt' / i / cal
4. hy'' / giene
   hy'' / gi / e / nist *or* hy'' / gie / nist *or* hy / gie' / nist
   hy / gi / en'' / ic *or* hy / gi'' / en / ic
   hy / gi / en'' / i / cal / ly
5. hyp / no' / sis
   hyp' / no / tize
   hyp' / no / tist
   hyp' / no / tism

4. Split Vowels

ia

1. Syl vi a
2. Cyn thi a
3. hys te ri a *or*
   hys ter i a
4. dys lex i a
5. Syr i a
6. en cy clo pe di a

180

1. Wy o ming
2. To ky o
3. Hy att
4. cy a nide
5. pol y es ter
6. gym na si um

Dictionary Marks and Less-Common Words

1. Learning the Markings with Words You Know

1. my
2. hymn
3. Lynn
4. dry
5. spry
6. style

2. Writing Less-Common Words

1. tyrant
2. hysterics
3. Pyrex
4. enzyme
5. thyroid
6. stylus
7. polyp
8. larynx
9. syringe
10. onyx
11. vinyl
12. pylon

1. pyramids
2. synthetic
3. dynasty
4. polygamy
5. asylum
6. anonymous
7. hydrogen
8. synagogue
9. homonyms
10. synonym
11. sycamore
12. symbolic

Handling *y* Words . . .Lightly

Confusing Business Names

(Answers may vary.)

General Dynamics
Hygienetics
Envirodyne Engineers
Hydroflo Systems
Symbolics, Inc.
Cytrix Corp.

Lytton Industries
Cybertronics
Teledyne
Industrial Analysts
Unisys

Odd Word Out

1. Clyde, female names
2. tyrant, jobs
3. crystal, plants
4. Kathryn, male names
5. amethysts, man-made materials
6. Wyoming, ailments
7. Senator Byrd, animals
8. Log Cabin Syrup, cleaning products
9. symptoms, music
10. Tylenol, places

Problem Solving

Alliance for the Mentally Ill
Sudden Infant Death Syndrome
Lyme Disease Support Group
Gamblers Anonymous Support Group
Adult Dyslexic Group
Parents Anonymous

Sources of City and Village Names

Butterfly **n**
Onyx **n**
Holly Hills **n**
Wytheville **p**
Fordyce **p**
Cyprus Gardens **n**
Ypsilanti **p**
Sylvester **p**
Bryan **p**
Tysons Corner **p**

Gettysburg **p**
Dyersburg **p**
Gypsum **n**
Myers Corners **p**
Tyrone **p**
Rye **n**
Tyler **p**
Lynchburg **p**
Cynthiana **p**
Sin Deny

Music: Groups or Single Performers

Bob Dylan, Crystal Gayle, Alyson Williams, Loretta Lynn, Leontyne Price, Cyndi Lauper, Jessye Norman, Lynyrd Skynyrd

Chapter 10. *ph* and *ch*

Sound and Spelling

1. The Sound of *ph (f)* as in **phone**

1. (Joseph)
2. Philip
3. nephew
4. trophy
5. Memphis
6. asphalt
7. orphan
8. Phyllis
9. Randolph
10. Rudolph
11. phony
12. Sophie

Longer, Common Words with *ph*

1. ele*ph*ant
2. al*ph*abet
3. ty*ph*oid
4. autogra*ph*
5. *ph*onora*ph*
6. *ph*otogra*ph*
7. so*ph*omore
8. saxo*ph*one
9. *ph*ysical

2. The Sound of *ch (k)* as in **school**

1. school
2. Chris
3. Christ
4. ache
5. chrome
6. scheme

181

Longer, Common Words with *ch* as in **school**

1. stoma**ch**
2. an**ch**or
3. e**ch**o
4. **ch**orus
5. Mi**ch**ael
6. s**ch**edule
7. **Ch**rysler
8. **Ch**ristmas
9. me**ch**anic

3. The Sound of *ch (sh)* as in **chef**

1. champagne
2. Chicago
3. Charlotte
4. Michigan
5. parachute
6. mustache
7. chandelier
8. chiffon

4. Spelling *ph* and *ch* Words

Add *ing*, *ed*, and *s*

1. phoning, phoned, phones
2. scheduling, scheduled, schedules
3. photographing, photographed, photographs
4. aching, ached, aches

Add *s* or *es*

1. choruses   2. phonographs   3. trophies

Syllables and Accents

1. Writing Words in Syllables

1. or′ ches tra
2. phar′ ma cy
3. chem′ is try
4. char′ ac ter
5. schol′ ar ship
6. pre Christ′ mas
7. sym′ pho ny
8. at′ mos phere
9. pho′ ni ness
10. ste nog′ ra pher
11. syph′ i lis
12. non phys′ i cal
13. em′ pha size
14. tech′ ni cal

2. Writing Related Words

1. chor′al
2. characteris′tics
3. atmospher′ic
4. scholas′tic
5. phar′macist

4. Word Building

1. al′/pha/bet
   al′/pha/bet/ize
   al/pha/bet′/i/cal
   al/pha/bet′/i/cal/ly
2. em′/pha/size
   em′/pha/sis
   em/phat′/ic

3. pho′/to/graph
   pho/tog′′/ra/phy
   pho/tog′′/ra/pher
4. chem′/ist
   chem′/i/cals
   chem′/is/try
   chem/mo/ther′′/a/py
5. me/chan′/ic
   me/chan′′/i/cal
   mech′/an/ize
6. tech′/ni/cal
   tech/nol′′/o/gy
   tech/ni/cal′′/i/ty

5. Split Vowels

        f
1. (geography   ge og ra phy)
        f
2. biography   bi og ra phy
      f   f
3. Philadelphia   Phil a del phi a
      k
4. psychiatrist   psy chi a trist
        f
5. diaphragm   di a phragm
   k
6. chaos   cha os
    k
7. trachea   tra che a
     f
8. diphtheria   diph the ri a *or*
   diph ther i a

Dictionary Marks and Less-Common Words

1. Learning the Markings with Words You Know

1. Joseph
2. nephew
3. Chris
4. orphan
5. scheme
6. ache
7. Philip
8. photo
9. chrome
10. Ralph
11. Christ
12. asphalt

2. Writing Less-Common Words

ph (f) as in **phone**

1. dolphin
2. physics
3. phonics
4. phosphates
5. graphics
6. hemisphere
7. esophagus
8. sapphire
9. hyphens
10. siphon
11. emphysema
12. paragraph

ch (k) as in **school**

1. cholera
2. chloride
3. chiropractor
4. psychology
5. architect
6. chloroform
7. monarch
8. chromosomes
9. chronic
10. strychnine
11. cholesterol
12. bronchitis

ch (sh) as in **Michigan**

1. pistachio
2. parachute
3. echelon
4. chaperone
5. champagne
6. chandelier

Handling *ph* and *ch* Words . . . Lightly

Books, Light Entertainment?

(Answers will vary.)

Phantom Cowboy

The Seven Sapphires of Mardi Gras

Eddie Murphy's Funny Stories

Moonlight Charade

The Triumph of Love

Who Wears Blue Chiffon, Anyway?

Parachutes and Kisses

The Chronicle of a Funny Man

The Mystery of Phoenix

Agatha Christie's murder mysteries

The Trophy

Echoes from Her Past

The Chicago Loop Murder

Ailments

stomach ulcers, syphilis, bronchitis, hydrophobia shots, chronic headache, diphtheria, emphysema, phobias about high places, typhoid fever, allergies to chemicals, choosing a good chiropractor, melancholic, blue feelings

Odd Word Out

1. atmosphere, reading and writing
2. photographs, animals
3. Chevrolets, jobs
4. parachute, music
5. emphasis, chemicals

New Company Names

(Answers may vary.)

Chemlawn, Cholestech, Techrep, Graphink, Dynatech, The Health Pharm, Synchron, Acoustech, Chemtreat

School District Names

(Answers may vary.)

White Elephant, Ephrata, Scholastica, Pumphrey, Zephyrville, Orphan's Gift, Olyphant, Jericho

Chapter 11. More Spellings of the *sh* Sound

Sound and Spelling

1. The *cia* and *tia* Spelling of the *sh* Sound

ci	tia
1. (special)	1. partial
2. facial	2. martial
3. racial	3. initial
4. social	4. palatial
5. Marcia	5. essential

2. The *cie* and *tie* Spelling of the *sh* Sound

1. ancient
2. deficient
3. efficient
4. sufficient
5. conscience
6. patient
7. patience

3. The *tion* and *sion* Spelling of the *sh* Sound

ti	si
1. action	1. session
2. function	2. pension
3. portion	3. tension

4. The *tious* and *cious* Spelling of the *sh* Sound

ti	ci
1. cautious	1. spacious
2. nutritious	2. conscious
3. flirtatious	3. suspicious

5. Spelling Common Suffixes / Endings with the *sh* Sound

Add *ing* and *ed*

1. mentioning, mentioned
2. cautioning, cautioned
3. functioning, functioned
4. stationing, stationed

Add *ly*

1. racially
2. socially
3. patiently
4. essentially
5. efficiently
6. consciously
7. nutriously
8. suspiciously

183

Syllables and Accents

1. Writing Words in Syllables

1. com mer′ cial
2. pres i den′ tial
3. com ple′ tion
4. de li′ cious
5. su per sti′ tious
6. dis crim i na′ tion
7. in sti tu′ tion
8. pro mo′ tion

2. Prefixes / Beginnings and Suffixes / Endings Syllables

1. so cial ize
2. non ra cial
3. es pe cial ly
4. im par tial
5. un con scious
6. spe cial ist
7. in ef fi cient
8. in suf fi cient
9. im pa tient
10. an ti so cial
11. con di tion al
12. mis sion ar y

3. Matching Related Words

tia and **cia** Words

1. musi′cian
2. magi′cian
3. offi′cial
4. judi′cial
5. creden′tials
6. finan′cial
7. politi′cian
8. residen′tial
9. mili′tia
10. electri′cian
11. benefi′cial
12. substan′tial

tion and **sion** Words

1. admis′sion
2. resigna′tion
3. invita′tion
4. informa′tion
5. expan′sion
6. execu′tion
7. occupa′tion
8. posses′sion
9. proposi′tion
10. impres′sion

4. Split Vowels

cia, tia, ia, cie

1. ap pre′ ci ate
2. as so′ ci ate
3. in i′ ti ate
4. of fi′ ci ate
5. ne go′ ti ate
6. pe di a tri′ cian
7. con sci en′ tious
8. ben e fi′ ci ar y

tion and **sion**

1. cre a′ tion
2. rec re a′ tion
3. vi o la′ tion
4. ra di a′ tion
5. ap pre ci a′ tion
6. in i ti a′ tion
7. ne go ti a′ tion
8. as so ci a′ tion

Dictionary Marks and Less-Common Words

1. Learning the Markings with Words You Know

1. spacious
2. ancient
3. pension
4. partial
5. nation
6. patient

2. Writing More Difficult Words

cia, **tia**

1. confidential
   mortician
2. technician
   superficial
3. optician
4. penitentiary
5. physician
   potential

cious, tious, tien, cien

1. infectious
2. ferocious
3. vicious
4. contentious
5. ambitious
6. quotient

tion, sion

1. automation
2. comprehension
3. acceleration
4. precipitation
5. depletion
6. pollination
7. frustration
8. conservation
9. persecution
10. ignition

3. Out-of-Pattern and other Confusing Words

1. ocean
2. sugar
3. tissue
4. luxury
5. Russian
6. pressure
7. insurance
8. nauseous
9. anxious
10. complexion

Handling More *sh*-Sound Words . . . Lightly

Earning a Living

be a physician

be a pediatrician

be a politician

be a hair and nail specialist

sell insurance

be a labor negotiator

work as an X-ray technician

be a musician with "The Temptations"

be a recreation supervisor

be a park conservation officer

be a mathematician

sell residential property

be a mortician

serve as a church missionary

be a transmission specialist

be a social worker

be an auctioneer

Getting to Know You

(Answers will vary.)

patient gracious affectionate

compassionate appreciative conscientious

Books for Children

(Answers may vary.)

The Fire Station, Loudmouth Lucius, A Mouse Called Junction, Devotions in the Children's Hour, The Magician and Mr. Tree, The Tiny Patient, Patricia and the New Baby, I Can Be an Electrician, Alicia and the Peacock

Helpful and Political Organizations

(Answers may vary.)

Salvation Army **1-1** National Association for the Advancement of Colored People **P** National Organization of Women **p** Coalition Against the Death Penalty **P** Post-Polio Connection **1-1** Relationships Anonymous **1-1** Committee for Conscientious Objection **P** Air Pollution Control Association **P** People for Environmental Protection **P** Compassionate Friends (for parents of children who have died) **1-1** Childbirth Preparation Classes **1-1** Catholic Social Services **1-1** Congress for Racial Equality (CORE) **P** Post-Adoption Hotline **1-1** Project Transition (for mental patients) **1-1** Emotions Anonymous **1-1**

Chapter 12. The "Ghostly Consonants" and "Borrowed" Vowel Sounds

The "Ghostly" Consonants

1. The Sound of *ch* as in nature

1. (statue) ^ch	(stat ue)
2. saturate ^ch	sat u rate
3. century ^ch	cen tur y *or* cen tu ry
4. furniture ^ch	fur ni ture
5. adventure ^ch	ad ven ture
6. congratulate ^ch	con grat u late
7. moisture ^ch	mois ture
8. spatula ^ch	spat u la

2. The Sound of *w* as in language

1. (genuine) ^w	4. persuade ^w
2. distinguish ^w	5. penguin ^w
3. bilingual ^w	6. extinguish ^w

ual	*uary*
(actual) ^w	February ^w
continual ^w	January ^w
factual ^w	mortuary ^w
manual ^w	obituary ^w
ritual ^w	sanctuary ^w
spiritual ^w	statuary ^w

185

3. Sound of *y* as in **Julia**

yə and *yəl*

Names of People: (Cecilia),
Daniel, Nathaniel, Virginia

Names of Places: Australia,
California, Pennsylvania, Virginia

Names of Plants: azalea,
gardenia, magnolia, petunia

yən, yər, yənt, yərd

yən as in **union, Italian:** bunion, champion, civilian, companion, communion, onion, opinion, rebellion

yər as in **senior, peculiar:** behavior, familiar, junior, savior

yənt as in **convenient:** brilliant, lenient

yərd as in **Spaniard:** billiard

4. The Sound of *zh* as in **vision**, **Asia**, **pleasure**

1. (exposure), leisure, measure,
   seizure, treasure
2. casual, visual
3. collision, division, explosion
4. Persia

5. The Sound of *k* as in **liquor**

1. masquerade
2. mosque
3. tourniquet
4. croquettes
5. lacquer
6. racquet
7. briquets
8. Roquefort
9. burlesque
10. conquer

6. Spelling with Common Endings

Add *ly*

1. casually
2. usually
3. brilliantly
4. naturally
5. leisurely
6. genuinely
7. conveniently
8. peculiarly

Add *ing*, *ed*, and *er*

1. treasuring, treasured, treasurer
2. questioning, questioned, questioner
3. extinguishing, extinguished, extinguisher

Add *es*

1. centuries   2. mortuaries   3. obituaries

7. Prefixes / Beginnings, Suffixes / Endings

1. persuasive
2. unchristian
3. indigestion
4. punctuality
5. reunion
6. displeasure
7. companionable
8. rebellious
9. familiar

The "Borrowed" Vowels

1. The Long *e* Sound Spelled by *i* as in **gasoline**, **police**, and **antique**

ine as in **gasoline**

(Christine), limousine, machine,
marine, Maxine, mezzanine,
nectarine, Pauline, routine,
sardine, tangerine, vaccine

ice as in **police** and *ique* as in **antique**

1. (an tique)
2. po lice
3. Clar ice
4. Mau rice
   or Maur ice
5. phy sique
6. u nique
7. tech nique
8. Ber nice

More Words with Long *e* spelled by *i*

1. mosquito
2. liter
3. fatigue
4. petite
5. debris
6. trio
7. paprika
8. zucchini
9. bikini
10. visa

2. The Final *e* as in **recipe**

Apache, apostrophe, catastrophe, karate, minestrone, posse, sesame, vigilante

3. Long *a* Spelled by *e*, as in **Café**, *ee* as in **fiancee**, *et* as in **Chevrolet**

Long *a* Sound of Final *e*, *ee*

$\bar{a}$ (café), communiqué $\bar{a}$, consommé $\bar{a}$,
divorcée $\bar{a}$, fiancée $\bar{a}$, rosé $\bar{a}$, purée $\bar{a}$, resumé $\bar{a}$

Long *a* Sound Spelled by *et*

$\bar{a}$ (ballet), bouquet $\bar{a}$, buffet $\bar{a}$,
cabaret $\bar{a}$, croquet $\bar{a}$, crochet $\bar{a}$,
filet $\bar{a}$, gourmet $\bar{a}$, ricochet $\bar{a}$, valet $\bar{a}$

Handling Words . . . Lightly

Rewards and Prizes

(Answers will vary.)

A week at Padré Island National Seashore

A trip to the old city of St. Augustine, FL

A stay at Yosemite National Park

A boat ride to Catalina Island, near Los Angeles

A voyage to Juneau, AK

Stretch limousine for a day

A tour of Magnolia Gardens, S. Carolina

A gift certificate at Café Daphne

A week at Wolverine Fitness Center

A trip to Statue of Liberty in NY harbor

An album "Grafitti Bridge" by Prince

$50 at Unique Film and Video Store

Books: Keep or Pass On?

(Answers will vary.)

Rebellious Heart

An Inconvenient Woman

Black Stallion

Masquerade

Union Forever

Situation Tragedy

The Corpse Had a Familiar Face

Unnatural Causes

Casino Royale

Visions of the Heart

Automobile Words

gasoline

machine tool

temperature

Buick Century

Champion spark plugs

technique

combustion engine

Festiva

precision timing

manual

Chevrolet

Capri

corrosion

Oldsmobile

Food-Service Words

nicotine, penguins, burlesque, erosion, anesthesia, morphine

Post Office and Travel Words

Australia, Philippines, Albuquerque, NM, San Bernardino, CA, Virginia, Indonesia, Mobile, AL, Santa Fe, NM, Bordeaux, Fr, Europe, Tunisia, California, Pennsylvania, Dominion of Canada, Beaumont, TX, Racine, WI, Puerto Rico

Law-Enforcement Words

police, ricochet bullets, questioning, vigilante, habitual criminal, behavior, explosion, rebellions, posse, catastrophe, casualties, civilian control, routine, collision, persuade

Famous Horses

(Answers may vary.)

Manuel, Polynesian, Jean Bereaud, Chateaugay, Genuine Risk, Pasteurized, Don Enrique, Foolish Pleasure, Panique, Comanche, Scottish Christian, Savior